WALKING WITH
THESSALONIANS

BECOME THE MAN GOD INTENDS YOU TO BE

Carriage
House
PUBLISHERS

A 30-DAY DEVOTIONAL
AND BIBLE STUDY

FRED J. PARRY

WALKING WITH THESSALONIANS

Published by
Carriage House Publishers
Library of Congress Control Number: 2022911362
Paperback ISBN: 979-8-9857824-2-4
eBook ISBN: 979-8-9857824-3-1
Cover design by Debbie Lewis
Interior design: Carolyn Preul
Theological Review: Patrick Miller
Technical Review: Gary Powell
Printed in the United States of America

ACKNOWLEDGMENT:

Special thanks to my friends Patrick Miller and Gary Powell for their expert guidance during the writing and editing of *Walking With Thessalonians*.

Patrick Miller (MDiv, Covenant Theological Seminary) is a pastor at The Crossing in Columbia, Missouri, where he oversees digital ministries. He offers cultural commentary and interviews with Christian thinkers on his podcast Truth Over Tribe, as well as devotions on his podcast Ten Minute Bible Talks. He's the author of Truth Over Tribe: *Pledging Allegiance to the Lamb, Not the Donkey or the Elephant* (David C. Cook). He is married to Emily and they have two kids. You can follow him on Twitter @PatrickKMiller_.

Gary Powell is the founding pastor at The Revolution Church in Columbia, Missouri. He ministers to those who need healing and equips the believer through simple faith and belief in the Word to effectively do the same. He is married to Audra and they have three kids. You can learn more about The Revolution at revolutioncolumbia.com.

For those brave women and men who were bold enough to plant a seed in my mind about the amazing grace and love that comes from a personal relationship with Jesus Christ. Your relentless pursuit over the course of nearly four decades has inspired me to pay it forward, embracing our savior's Great Commission.

For those who persisted, and never gave up ... I am eternally grateful for your love and discipleship.

....

"And as for you, brothers and sisters,
never tire of doing what is good."

(2 Thessalonians 3:13 NIV)

CONTENTS

For more information on using this book for a group study,
please visit **www.FredParry.Life** to access study materials,
handouts, and other useful information.

INTRODUCTION

JUST GETTING STARTED

"Therefore encourage one another and build each other up, just as in fact you are doing." (1 Thessalonians 5:11 NIV)

When I first made the decision to dedicate my life to Christ, I had the false expectation of being completely transformed the minute I emerged from the murky water at my baptism ceremony. For reasons that now seem absurd, I fully expected to instantly become a new man. As if someone had waved a magic wand, I assumed that my sinful desires of lust, pride, and greed would simply dissipate into the ether. I was sorely disappointed just a few hours later when some trivial circumstance in my life triggered an angry outburst.

As the days and weeks progressed, I discovered that very little had changed in my behavior. My emotions, desires, and proclivity towards sinful things had not changed in the least. The only thing that my baptism changed was the promise that God had made to me that I would enjoy eternal life with him when I accepted his gift of salvation. By faith, I received the Holy Spirit, who promises to work by God's grace to transform my life. But that is a process that takes a lifetime, not a moment. Unfortunately, I was getting off to a rough start in my new journey.

As you will see in Paul's letters to the Thessalonians, new believers need some very specific guidance to help them grow and mature in the early stages of their relationship with Christ. Every one of us needs encouragement. Whether it comes from a parent, coach, pastor, or a complete stranger, we all thrive on the reassurance that comes with an encouraging word or a pat on the back. This is especially important for new Christians. Because of our wounded nature and our initial apprehension toward putting our complete trust in God, the first few steps of living a Christ-centered life can seem very uncertain. If you're like me, you might be starting off with unreasonable expectations or perhaps you've not quite figured out how to incorporate the dynamics of this new relationship into the tidy compartments of your complicated life.

Surprisingly, Paul's letters to the Thessalonians taught me that followers of Christ may need to experience a degree of suffering to truly achieve the spiritual maturity needed to fully understand the gift we've been given. Though subtler and less violent than what Paul's early believers encountered, new believers, even today, face forms of persecution related to their decision to follow Christ. When I first converted, even my best friends would ridicule me about the inconsistencies in my life. They would call me a hypocrite for saying one thing and doing another. Instead of encouraging me along the path, they made me insecure and doubtful.

Instead of getting new friends, I became determined to prove
to them that I was capable of becoming a better person and
turning my life around. These same friends would accuse me
of being a "pretender" and those words had a painful sting to
them. The only way I could prove them wrong was to find a
way to resist temptation, be intentional about my walk, and
draw myself closer to God. I didn't do this to earn God's favor.
I already had that in Christ. Instead, I resisted temptation
by the power of his grace and spirit. Again, this is a faltering
process full of forgiveness and prayer. Two steps forward. One
step back. Two steps forward. One step back. You get the idea.

Of course, there are people in various parts of the world who
face levels of persecution far worse than ridicule for their
religious beliefs. We've all seen videos of Christians being
tortured and decapitated by members of the Islamic State.
We also know that being a Christian is forbidden in many
countries controlled by oppressive regimes. What's required of
us as modern Christians in America is a cakewalk compared
to the sacrifice faced by others around the world. For that
reason, it should be much easier for us to answer God's call to
stand up to evil, wherever it may exist. Satan has put a bullseye
on the back of new believers because he feels threatened by
the growth of God's kingdom. Paul reminds us that we have an
obligation to nurture, comfort, and help these new Christians
grow in their faith.

If you're a new believer, you can help yourself by seeking
out a small group of men who will envelop you, hold you
accountable, and give you the strength that only comes

in numbers. Every man needs the fellowship of Christian brothers who will be there to protect and encourage him if you're willing to let them into your life. Don't try to navigate life's complicated turns by yourself. Most importantly, avoid isolation and commit yourself to vulnerability and transparency in the presence of other men.

In each chapter of 1 Thessalonians, Paul reminds new believers that they should be motivated and encouraged by the promise of the second coming of Christ. Knowing that the living and dead, who have confessed their faith to God, will one day be reunited in God's kingdom should be a powerful incentive for living a life filled with service and compassion for others. The promise that Christians have been given for eternal life in heaven is the prize on which our eyes and hearts should be constantly focused.

In 2 Thessalonians, Paul goes to great lengths to educate his new believers on the reality of spiritual warfare. Satan, himself, has a deeply vested interest in driving a wedge between us and God. Paul warns us to be on the lookout for evil and to stand firm when we are confronted. We should never underestimate what Satan will do to destroy our lives. God allows Satan to give us trials so that we can strengthen our faith as a result of our struggles and challenges. When bad things happen, our faith and perseverance help build character and that is what ultimately makes us more spiritually mature.

In the end, Paul tells us to rejoice and be thankful for all things and to pray continually. The Holy Spirit uses these everyday practices to produce the fruit that leads us to a more joyful and meaningful life. You already have God's love and favor in Christ. His love is expressed to us in the gift of his Spirit, who empowers us to grow in holiness over time. This is a group project! The Spirit works, by grace, through our work.

Fred J. Parry

MY PRAYER

God, I pray today that you will open my heart and give me the clarity of mind to fully comprehend and embrace the wisdom that comes from Paul's letters to the Thessalonians. Let me lean into your call to persevere through each of life's challenges, to grow constantly in my faith, and to build your kingdom by encouraging new believers who now walk the path I followed when I first met you. Let me rejoice and be thankful for all things. For this, I pray in the name of your Son, Jesus Christ. Amen.

HOW TO USE THIS BOOK

W*alking with Thessalonians: Become The Man God Intends You To Be* is designed to serve the dual purpose of being both a daily devotional and study guide for 1 Thessalonians and 2 Thessalonians. While the book is structured to be used over a six-week period, I would encourage you to use it at a pace that is most comfortable for you.

Each of the daily devotions is inspired by a passage in Paul's letters to the Thessalonians. From these passages, I have found themes that can guide us in our daily walk to become more like Jesus. From these eight short chapters, you will discover important teachings from Paul on courage, perseverance, gratitude, and what it means to stand firm in the face of the enemy. These devotionals were written as responses to my own personal understanding of how a particular passage spoke to me. The goal of any Bible Study is to find the correct interpretation which leads to a variety of applications. That, in itself, is rightly handling the word of truth (2 Timothy 2:15).

If you're like me, you'll get a new insight or meaning each time you read one of these passages and not because the Bible's meaning has changed, but because we, as individuals, have changed since the last time we were there. We've become more aware of a different aspect of our lives, and this scripture now speaks to us in a new way. We are more teachable than we were before. The Bible takes us on where we are, and God uses his Word to lead us to greater maturity and a broader perspective. The Bible is as deep as we are and deeper still.

I would suggest approaching each devotional in prayer, asking God for clarity of mind and focus with the hope that the day's message resonates with you in some meaningful way.

Once you've read the devotional, you'll find the following tools at the end of each reading to help you get the most meaning out of the day's message:

- A reference to scripture outside Thessalonians that will reinforce and add context to the day's message.

- Next, you'll have two short questions designed to help you apply that day's lesson to your life.

- Finally, you'll find a call to contemplation, which is intended as a prompt for journaling or small group discussions. It's an excellent opportunity to explore and record your feelings as they relate to the day's message.

Before you begin this study, I would encourage you to read through the New International Version (NIV) of 1 Thessalonians and 2 Thessalonians. As you work your way through the study, go back and read these chapters again. To gain a better understanding of the context of each day's passage, I would encourage you to refer to the full text as often as you can to fully understand the cultural, historical, and literary context of the events surrounding each passage.

I hope that you'll find these devotionals to be useful and relevant in your daily walk. My prayer is that the wisdom that comes from Paul's letters to the Thessalonians will guide you in your journey to lead a more fulfilling and Christ-centered life.

FJP

BACKGROUND

THE APOSTLE PAUL

Paul was born in the city of Tarsus, a major city in eastern Cilicia on the trade route between Syria and Asia Minor, which was located in the same geographical region as modern-day Turkey. Born the son of a Pharisee and in the ancestral lineage of the Tribe of Benjamin, Paul enjoyed the unique distinction of being a Jew and the privilege of being a Roman citizen. He could speak Hebrew but his native tongue was Koine Greek. Paul was educated at the prestigious Rabbinical school taught by Gamaliel, who was one of the most influential rabbis in the history of ancient Judaism.

Paul is considered to be among the most important figures in the history and growth of Christianity. He is the author of 13 of the 27 books in the New Testament. While there is some scholarly debate as to the complete authenticity of some of the books in the New Testament, experts acknowledge that at least seven of the 13 books from Paul are undisputed as authentic works of Paul. 1 Thessalonians is an undisputed letter, there is some debate over 2 Thessalonians. While the debate over 2 Thessalonians might interest scholars, it's helpful for you to know that there is strong evidence that Paul also wrote this letter, and most Christians today believe he did.

PAUL'S CONVERSION

Readers of the New Testament first encounter Paul as "Saul of Tarsus." Though Saul was a tentmaker by trade, he was also a fervent persecutor of early Christians. In Acts 9:1-22, we read of Saul traveling from Jerusalem to Damascus during his crusade to arrest disciples when he encounters the resurrected Jesus in a great light. During this experience, Jesus reveals to Saul that he is Lord and that persecuting his followers is the same as persecuting the Lord Jesus and is, in effect, fighting against God. N.T. Wright conjectures that during this journey, Paul was repeating a prayer, used by many serious Jews in his day, requesting a visionary experience of God. An answer to that prayer was surprising enough, but seeing Jesus in the place of Yahweh literally reconfigured Paul's worldview.

During this encounter, Saul was temporarily blinded by the light that surrounded the vision of Jesus but, in spite of this, he traveled on to Damascus where he remained blind for three days. Saul took no food or water for this period and stayed in a constant state of prayer until approached by a disciple named Ananias. Ananias told Saul that he had been sent by Jesus to restore his sight and assured Saul that the Lord would fill him with the Holy Spirit. Once Saul's sight was restored, he was immediately baptized and became a fervent believer in Jesus Christ.

PAUL'S MISSIONARY TRIPS

Following his baptism, Paul went on to Arabia and Damascus and began to preach that Jesus was the Messiah. It was soon thereafter that he began to be persecuted for his teachings. Around A.D. 37, nearly three years after his conversion, Paul traveled to Jerusalem where he met for 15 days with James, the half-brother of Jesus, and the apostle Peter. Paul used these meetings to learn more about the life of Jesus and to report on his efforts in preaching about the Kingdom of God and Jesus the Messiah. Over time, Paul became known as the "Apostle to the Gentiles," while Peter would be known as the "Apostle to the Jews."

Soon after Paul met with James and Peter, he returned to his hometown of Tarsus to preach until he was invited by Barnabas to go and teach at the rapidly growing church in Antioch. It was there where Paul began to build a network of house churches where the earliest Christians would gather at the homes of other followers until the size of the group forced them to divide into smaller groups. Antioch was also the first place where Jewish-Gentile churches took root. In Acts 15, Paul and Barnabas meet with the apostles and discuss whether Gentile converts needed to be circumcised and conform to other strict Jewish rituals. With limited resources, Paul and Barnabas often relied on the generosity of their converts for food and housing. In A.D. 47, Paul returned to Jerusalem with Barnabas and brought famine relief contributed by the early churches they had started. In doing so, Paul was, perhaps, the earliest pioneer of missionary work that would be done by churches throughout the coming centuries.

Paul and Barnabas then set out from Antioch on the first of three mission trips where they visited Cyprus and Galatia. It was around this time that Saul began to be more commonly referred to as Paul. Historians speculate that Paul was actually Saul's Roman name and that the names may have been used interchangeably so that he could more easily relate to a diverse variety of audiences.

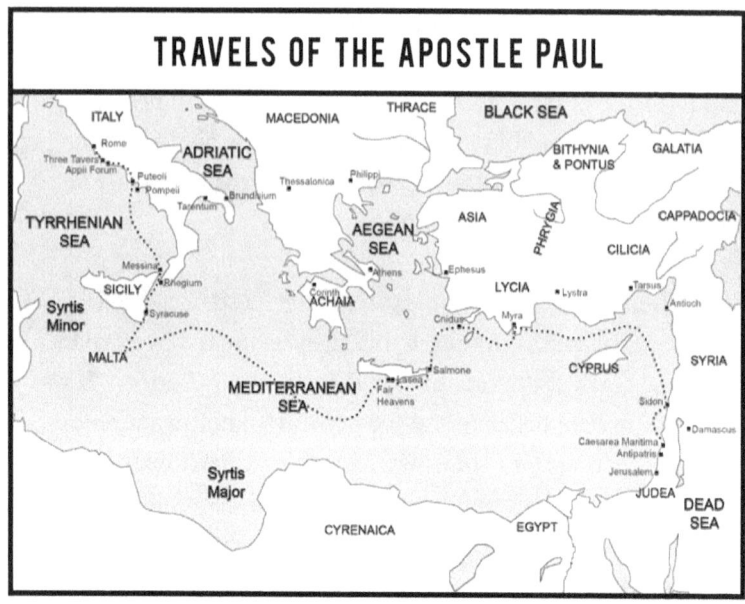

TRAVELS OF THE APOSTLE PAUL

Copyright 2022. Fred Parry

After parting ways with Barnabas in Antioch, Paul chose Silas (Silvanus) to accompany him to Syria and Cilicia in an effort to reinforce Paul's work with the churches he had previously established there. Their travels led them to Derbe and to Lystra, where they met Timothy, who was well-respected in the area. He was the son of a Jewish woman and a Greek father. As the three traveled through Phrygia and Galatia, Paul had a vision one night of a man from Macedonia pleading for them to come to that region. The next morning, they departed immediately, sailing from Troas on a course to Samothrace, Neapolis and then to Philippi. When Paul exorcised the demons from a slave girl, he and Silas were imprisoned in Phillipi for a short time. Once released from captivity they left Philippi. From there they traveled through Amphipolis and Apollonia before arriving in Thessalonica.

THE SIGNIFICANCE OF THESSALONICA

Thessalonica was the home of an important dockyard situated on the harbor of the Thermaic Gulf in the northwest corner of the Aegean Sea near the junction of the Egnatian Way and the road that led north to the Danube. Built by the Romans as their primary route east to Byzantium, the Egnatian Way was nearly 700 miles long at the time. The roadway was nearly 20 feet wide and paved with large stone slabs topped off by a hardened layer of sand. It traversed several mountain passes and river gorges providing travelers a direct connection between Rome and the Aegean Sea.

Thessalonica thrived because of its location along this major trade route to the east into Asia and west to Rome, becoming a city known for its prosperity and cultural activity. Located 100 miles southwest of Philippi, Thessalonica eventually became the capital of the Roman province of Macedon. Thessalonica was a thriving city of nearly 200,000 citizens in Macedonia in Northern Greece. The city still exists but is now known as Thessaloniki.

Paul's trip to Thessalonica was significant because it was the beginning of spreading the gospel from Asia to Europe. Philippi was the first city in Europe to hear the gospel from Paul. Tragically, Paul's time in Thessalonica was cut short by mob-led persecution. He fled the region and traveled on to Berea, but angry mobs there forced him to again move on to Athens for a short time. Paul eventually settled in Corinth.

In 1 Corinthians 2:3, we learn that Paul had become fearful and very discouraged with the fruits of his missionary work. He deeply regretted leaving his new believers before they were established in their faith. The imprisonment, persecution, and treatment by angry mobs had taken a toll on Paul. He became very concerned about the churches he had planted and worried about their viability. While in Berea, Paul sent Silas and Timothy back to Thessalonica to check on this new church.

THE LETTERS TO THESSALONICA

Paul's first letter to the Thessalonians is also one of the earliest letters we have from him to any church. This means that 1 Thessalonians is older than the gospels of Matthew, Mark, Luke, and John as well as every other New Testament book with the exceptions of Galatians and James.

Paul's letters to the Thessalonians were written nearly 20 years after the resurrection of Christ (A.D. 51-52) from the city of Corinth. Paul's purpose in writing was to offer encouragement for the new converts he left behind. He wanted to give them instruction so they could persevere through the trials they faced. Many of the Gentiles that were now members of the new church had come from paganism and idolatry and Paul wanted to give them reassurance as they adjusted to a new way of thinking about the world. More than anything, Paul wanted to offer them hope of the promised return of Christ to help these new believers push through the persecution they were enduring.

1 THESSALONIANS

Paul's first letter to Thessalonica was prompted by the good news he had received from Silas and Timothy upon their return from Macedonia. They reported to Paul that the new church in Thessalonica had continued to grow and thrive during the months following Paul's escape. Paul was elated to hear this news and immediately wrote the letter. Paul used this opportunity to encourage the new believers in Thessalonica and to fortify them in the basic doctrine of Christianity. Paul knew that this new church had faced an abundance of persecution and he wanted to praise these new believers for their fidelity to the gospel and their steadfast response to difficult circumstances. The good news from Thessalonica gave Paul a much-needed boost of encouragement and was a turning point in his ministry, which led to a renewed sense of energy and fruitfulness in his work at Corinth.

Paul's first letter to the Thessalonians is deeply personal in nature and does not specifically address church doctrine until the final two chapters. This letter includes scripture's first reference to the Rapture. In Timothy's report back to Paul, he indicated that there was great confusion regarding the end times and, as a result, many members of the new church were becoming disheartened and were beginning to question Paul's other teachings. In response, Paul goes to great lengths to explain what will take place during Christ's second coming and makes clear that the timing of Christ's return cannot be known. Paul's intentions were to reassure new Christians and to encourage young pastors through this letter. He also wanted to discredit the false teachings of those who were intentionally misleading those who were still young in their faith. Finally, Paul wanted to address those new believers who had stopped working in anticipation of the return of Christ, by reinforcing the message that hard work, especially

that which benefits others, is an essential element of being a true
follower of Christ.

The deeper you dive into the subject of the Rapture, you'll
discover that there are a lot of misconceptions around the topic.
My friend Patrick Miller, who is a fellow author and pastor,
wrote a thoughtful essay explaining what the Bible actually says
about the Rapture. Feel free to disagree with his perspective, but
I think it's worth considering his thoughts before you make up
your mind. You owe it to yourself to explore different viewpoints
but ultimately the truth will be found in God's word. You'll find
Patrick's essay on pages 97 to 101 in this book.

2 THESSALONIANS

Paul's second letter to Thessalonica is the shortest epistle that
Paul wrote to any church. It was written within six months of his
first letter and was likely made necessary due to a second report
that concerned Paul: the Thessalonian church continued to be
confused about the return of Jesus. In addition to correcting false
doctrine, Paul wanted to again ease the minds about the timing of
the second coming of Christ. Many had misinterpreted Paul's first
epistle to imply that the return of Christ was imminent. When the
persecution intensified and fellow churchgoers began to die, even
by natural causes, many worried that they would not be resurrected,
and became impatient waiting for Jesus's return. Paul's second letter
implored the new believers to maintain their faith and to be steadfast
in their courage even in the light of harsh and persistent persecution.
Paul assured his readers that God would justly punish those who
had persecuted members of his new church, and all who died before
Christ's return would be resurrected.

Biblical scholars point to the influence of Jewish Apocalyptic writings in Paul's teachings to the early church. These writings focus on the righteousness and repentance that must come before end times occur and were likely part of Paul's early education in the Rabbinical school led by Gamaliel. Paul warns his readers that the false teachings, lawlessness, disorder, and rebellion taking place were the work of Satan.

Another key theme in 2 Thessalonians relates to the necessity to suffer through the trials and frustration that came with the persecution these new believers were experiencing. Paul wanted his readers to focus their eyes on the future, when they would be reunited with Christ and when their suffering would end. He wanted to remind them that they would be strengthened by the adversity they were encountering and that they would not grow weary while doing good works for the benefit of others.

In the end, Paul encouraged his readers to take heart in the great promises of the gospel. The anticipation of Christ's return would be like water for a thirsty soul. Paul told them to continue to grow and mature through their suffering but do so with the hope of what lies ahead. Paul instructed his new believers to pray without ceasing, give thanks in all things, and to stand firm in the face of the enemy. As history now shows, Paul's reassurance to his new believers in Thessalonica would have a great impact on the growth of Christ's church.

THE CAPTIVITY EPISTLES

So what happened to Paul after he wrote his letter to Thessalonica?

Throughout his ministry life, Paul was jailed on numerous occasions and placed under house arrest for extended periods. It was during these periods that Paul crafted several of his letters to the churches he had planted. Because these letters were written while he was imprisoned, they are often referred to as the "Captivity Epistles."

In Acts 16:16-34, we read that Paul and Silas were imprisoned in Philippi for disturbing the peace after casting a demon out of a slave girl. While imprisoned, a sudden earthquake brought down the walls of the jail. Paul and Silas made the conscious decision to not escape, and this led to what would become a trusted relationship with their jailer, who became a follower of Christ. In A.D. 57, Paul returned to Jerusalem and was soon arrested and jailed for taking a Gentile too far into the precincts of the temple. These were false accusations, based on faulty assumptions, but they caused enough upheaval to gain Roman attention (Acts 22:29).

During his captivity in Jerusalem, Paul defended his actions before the Sanhedrin. His testimony divided the Sadducees and Pharisees who had strong disagreements over whether Paul had broken any laws. Roman authorities then took Paul, with an armed escort to Caesarea for higher officials to hear the case. Paul remained there for several years, and despite his innocence, was not released. Biblical tradition reports that a Roman official was trying to extort a bribe from him (Acts 24:26). Finally, exasperated, Paul asked to make an appeal to Caesar himself. After his request was reluctantly granted, Paul was placed on a ship, as a prisoner, to sail to Rome. On that voyage, he was shipwrecked on the island of Malta for three months where he performed miracles and continued to preach the Word of God.

When Paul finally arrived in Rome, he was placed under house arrest but was allowed to continue preaching without interruption from authorities. During this time, Paul wrote his letters to the Philippians, Ephesians, Colossians, and Philemon. Upon his release, it is believed that Paul then traveled to Spain where he wrote his letters to Timothy and Titus.

PAUL'S DEATH SENTENCE

In A.D. 64, Paul returned to Rome where he was martyred. While little has been written regarding the details surrounding Paul's death, tradition has it that Paul was sentenced to death by the Roman Emperor Nero. Paul's death sentence came shortly after a large portion of Rome, filled mostly with tenements for the poor, burned in a fire. Nero blamed the fire on Christians, though Roman documents suggest that Nero started the fire himself to clear the area for a building project. Because Paul was a Roman citizen, he was exempt from death by crucifixion. Instead, he was decapitated by a sword. In the end, Paul died because of his faith. In his final writings, it was clear that Paul was ready and willing to die for Christ; giving his last breath for the cause of helping the first generation of Christians understand that sacrifice was an integral part of following Christ.

"Instead, we were like young children among you. Just as a nursing mother cares for her children, so we cared for you. Because we loved you so much, we were delighted to share with you not only the gospel of God but our lives as well."

(1 Thessalonians 2:7-8)

WEEK 1

LABOR OF LOVE

We always thank God for all of you and continually mention you in our prayers. We remember before our God and Father your work produced by faith, your labor prompted by love, and your endurance inspired by hope in our Lord Jesus Christ. (1 Thessalonians 1:2-3)

H ave you ever loved a job so much that it never felt like work? Unfortunately, not enough of us can stake that claim. Perhaps your job is mundane and seemingly unimportant in the grand scheme of things. However, if you can find meaning and value in your work, you're much more likely to love your work. In the Book of James, we are reminded of the relationship between our faith and our work on behalf of others. James taught us that faith without works is dead. Perhaps the opposite is true as well. When our work is not inspired by faith, we are far less productive.

Is there a connection between your faith and your productivity? In Paul's letter to the Thessalonians, Paul commends his audience for the passion they have put into their work in spreading God's word. He notes that their work seems to be inspired by their faith and that their love is the essential element driving their labor for the benefit of God's kingdom. Paul reminded his readers that their hope would give them the endurance to push through the hardships and persecution that might have otherwise distracted them. We are reminded in this passage that those who truly love Christ are willing to suffer with him. The Thessalonians were a shining example of that. There were many temptations for them to abandon their faith, but they forged ahead and were steadfast in their love for God.

Ancient Greek had multiple words for "love." One of those words, agape, is the type of love that inspires self-sacrifice. When we are willing to give all we have for the benefit of others, denying ourselves to the point of exhaustion, the work we do suddenly becomes rewarding in immeasurable ways. Thanks to the gift of salvation, we do not have to toil or labor to earn God's grace. Because of that, we can be intentional in devoting our energies to telling others about Jesus and all that he has done for us. To truly labor for God, we may be required to sacrificially risk our comfort and security in his service by being willing to exchange our sweat and blood for the benefit of growing his kingdom. When we put God and others first, our labor will become fulfilling. The overwhelming joy we experience as a result will make us even more effective in our endeavors as disciples for Christ.

MY PRAYER

God, let the focus of my work be dedicated to serving you and others so that I can find fulfillment in every endeavor. Let my work be produced by faith, my labor prompted by love and my endurance fueled by the hope in my salvation. For these things, I pray in the name of your son, Jesus Christ. Amen.

READ: JAMES 2:18-26

QUESTION #1: Do you recognize a connection between sacrificial love and productivity in your work?

QUESTION #2: In what area of your life are you most reluctant to sacrifice comfort and security for the benefit of serving others?

CONTEMPLATE

Write about a job you've held that you found rewarding or fulfilling. What aspects of the job made it fulfilling? In what ways did it involve serving others?

LIVING OUT THE WORD

For we know, brothers and sisters loved by God, that he has chosen you, because our gospel came to you not simply with words but also with power, with the Holy Spirit and deep conviction. You know how we lived among you for your sake. (1 Thessalonians 1:4-5)

It has been said that God's truth will never make its way into our heads if it first doesn't make its way into our hearts. To read and understand what the Bible says is an important first step for us, but we can't expect to experience transformation in our lives until we actually start doing what the Bible says. In his letter to Thessalonica, Paul wanted to remind his audience that he, Timothy and Silas had not only preached the word of God, but they also lived it out. They set an example for others by living lives that honored God. Through their labor, daily conduct and self-sacrifice, they modeled what it meant to be a true Christian.

So what does a meaningful life built on Christian conduct look like? If you're still struggling to find meaning, fall back on the two basic things Jesus taught us in Matthew 22:36-40: love the Lord your God with all your heart and with all your soul and with all your mind, and secondly, love your neighbor as yourself. If you simply focus on those two things, you'll inevitably find yourself living out the word.

There will be times in our lives when we inadvertently fail to follow the examples laid out for us in the Bible. There will also be times when we witness stalwarts of the Christian faith fall in a very public way. Through our disappointment, we must focus our minds on the message rather than the messenger. God uses imperfect humans as his means for spreading the Gospel. When these humans fail, we should extend to them the grace that God has extended to us. Every now and then, each of us will eventually need someone to pick us up and dust us off. How we respond in those seasons of our lives will ultimately reveal whether our lives confirm or contradict that which we claim to believe.

MY PRAYER

God, give me the clarity of mind and wisdom to find meaning in the Gospel. Clear my mind of the distractions and prejudices so that I might notice those who are living out your Word. Let me grow to the point where my conduct, labor, and sacrifice illuminates all that comes from your word. Amen.

READ: COLOSSIANS 3:1-7

QUESTION #1: What part of your daily routine serves as a confirmation of your Christian faith?

QUESTION #2: In what ways is your personal conduct out of alignment with Christian conduct?

CONTEMPLATE

Recall a time when you ignored an important message because of your lack of confidence or respect for the messenger. Has the conduct of your life ever created a similar situation for someone else? Explain.

WHY NOT ME?

You became imitators of us and of the Lord, for you welcomed the message in the midst of severe suffering with the joy given by the Holy Spirit. (1 Thessalonians 1:6)

I n these verses, Paul acknowledges the suffering his friends are experiencing while spreading the news of God's kingdom. By God's grace, suffering and joy don't need to be mutually exclusive. He ensures that the two work in tandem for good. Our trials produce perseverance and our perseverance produces character. This character will produce hope in any situation, and that hope will never be put to shame. God doesn't use suffering or torment to teach us. We've already been redeemed in Jesus.

In Matthew 10:16-42, we learn of Jesus warning his disciples that they would be going out into a dangerous world where their faith would make them feel like sheep in a pack of wolves. Jesus knew that their suffering would strengthen them, making them more prepared and battle-ready for the challenges that lie ahead. While suffering never seems to be good on its own, God transforms the pain of suffering into something beneficial, and Paul wanted his readers in Thessalonica to know that truth.

In your life, good things will come from your despair and darkest moments, but only if the darkness presses you nearer to Jesus. With this knowledge, you can have the confidence to become bolder in your faith and more open to the self-sacrifice that is often required to lead a Christ-centered life. In times of trial, you must embrace the pain, knowing that it will eventually lead you to great things in your lives. You should rejoice in the fact that we are counted worthy of suffering for the expansion of God's kingdom.

MY PRAYER

God, help me to find the joy that exists in the midst of suffering and turmoil. Give me the perseverance I need to build my character so that I will find hope instead of despair. Let me be bold in faith, powered by the joy of the Holy Spirit so that I may serve your Kingdom today and every day moving forward. Amen.

READ: 1 PETER 1:5-10

QUESTION #1: In what part of your Christian journey have you experienced suffering or a seemingly insurmountable challenge? How did God help you through this experience?

QUESTION #2: Based on Paul's teachings, how will you respond the next time you encounter a significant trial in your life?

CONTEMPLATE

Recall a time in your life when your perseverance resulted in the strengthening of your character. How did this affect the outcome? How did it affect your sense of hope in dealing with future situations?

THE COURAGE TO BE BOLD

You know, brothers and sisters, that our visit to you was not without results. We had previously suffered and been treated outrageously in Philippi, as you know, but with the help of our God we dared to tell you his gospel in the face of strong opposition. (1 Thessalonians 2:1-2)

Prior to his arrival in Thessalonica, Paul had been imprisoned and had been subjected to brutal floggings and other forms of punishment. The persecution continued in Thessalonica. Despite the persistent abuse, Paul persevered. His enemies accused him of hypocrisy and false teachings and made every effort to undermine the work he had done in that region. The Holy Spirit gave Paul the power to endure and to be steadfast even while under attack. Paul's boldness was not reckless or impulsive but intentional and purposeful. Paul knew that if he were discredited, the Gospel he preached would also be called into question.

In today's culture, we often confuse boldness with brashness. It's important to know that even a shy and timid person can be bold in his or her faith. The goal is not to be overbearing or self-righteous about your faith, but rather to share the good news with gentleness and respect. Boldness is the opposite of cowardice, not kindness. No one gets gold stars from God by hiding their faith or by being a 'jerk for Jesus.' He wants us to share our faith persuasively, with gentleness and love. When someone asks us about the source of the hope and joy we exude in our daily lives, we must do it with gentleness and respect. (1 Pet. 3:15)

Becoming bold is not an instantaneous or overnight process. You can start with baby steps that will lead you in the right direction. Pray for the courage to speak out for what is right. Ask God to help you recognize when opportunities for discipleship present themselves. Most importantly, walk the walk. You can show others the benefits of a Christ-centered life without ever saying a word. They will recognize your joy and the compassion you have for others. They will see the presence of the Holy Spirit in you. Once we press through our fears, people will recognize it and be drawn to us because they know we are authentic ambassadors for Christ.

MY PRAYER

Heavenly Father, give me the courage to be bold when I need to be. Let me project the joy and hope that demonstrates my relationship with you and my genuine love for those around me. Give me the confidence and humility I need to encourage those who are seeking a deeper relationship with you. I pray for these things in the name of your son, Jesus. Amen.

READ: ACTS 4:13-31

QUESTION #1: What are the fears that prevent you from being bold in your faith?

QUESTION #2: What are the ways you can demonstrate your faith to others without saying a single word?

CONTEMPLATE

In what ways might you show others—in word and deed—the importance of your faith and the reason for your hope in Christ?

BE GENTLE

Instead, we were like young children among you. Just as a nursing mother cares for her children, so we cared for you. Because we loved you so much, we were delighted to share with you not only the gospel of God but our lives as well. (1 Thessalonians 2:7-8)

I f you grew up with brothers or you're now the father of sons, you know that boys can be rambunctious, rowdy and often out of control. In our youth, there were occasions when our mothers told us to "be gentle," like when holding a newborn infant or a small animal. Rarely did we hear those words pass through our father's lips. To the contrary, the fatherly advice we most often received from Dad was his encouragement from the sidelines or bleachers telling us to "run faster" or "hit harder!" Because the most meaningful reward systems in our adolescence were usually tied to our physical performance on the basketball court or football field, being gentle was the last thing on our minds.

Has much changed in your transition from teenager to adult? Is your masculinity still inextricably tied to hitting hard? Banging your fists on the table or roaring at extraordinary decibels when your favorite team makes the slightest movement towards the goal line? In our society, men rarely respect gentleness or hold it in high esteem. We were programmed to believe that being aggressive and assertive were the only ways to win the game of life. In the wake of this faulty belief system, many men have found themselves isolated, at a loss as to why their lives didn't go as planned. The apostle Paul could easily understand your predicament. He was a hard-hitting, ruthless persecutor of the church. But then something changed. He met Jesus and became someone who relied on gentleness and kindness to advance God's kingdom.

Paul encouraged his followers to be gentle with new Christians and to nurture their development the way a mother cares for her child. Paul teaches us that gentleness is a strong hand with a soft touch, showing compassion and meekness when dealing with others' weaknesses and faults. A gentle person can still speak truth into a painful situation but does so with an empathetic tone that allows the truth to be received in the manner intended. We are all recipients of the mercy and grace that are part of Christ's gentleness. As men, we should strive to extend this gift to others.

MY PRAYER

Father God, let me be the strong hand with a soft touch. Help me to abandon the aggressiveness that separates me from You. Let me model your patience, compassion, and kindness to all who call themselves your children. I pray for these things in the name your son, Jesus. Amen.

READ: EPHESIANS 4:1-8

QUESTION #1: What are the situations in your life where your gentleness might make a difference?

QUESTION #2: In what area of your life would a touch of gentleness allow you to speak truth into an uncomfortable situation?

CONTEMPLATE

Recall a time when someone used a gentle approach to make you think twice about your actions. What were the circumstances? Was that approach effective? Why or why not?

"Therefore, brothers and sisters, in all our distress and persecution we were encouraged about you because of your faith. For now we really live, since you are standing firm in the Lord."

(1 Thessalonians 3:7-8)

WEEK 2

THE POWER OF GOD'S WORD

And we also thank God continually because, when you received the word of God, which you heard from us, you accepted it not as a human word, but as it actually is, the word of God, which is indeed at work in you who believe. (1 Thessalonians 2:13)

I grew up in a household where the Bible was never opened. I suppose you could say that we were a "religious" family. We faithfully attended church every Sunday. I, along with my six siblings, participated in catechism classes every Saturday morning. Thanks to my aunt, who is a Catholic nun, we had access to a Bible because she gave one to our family for Christmas nearly every year. Nevertheless, I never cracked open the Bible until I was 45 years old. Even with all those years under my belt, it wasn't easy getting started. I would seek counsel from other believers on what I should be reading and then find a reason why that plan wasn't going to work for me. But once I finally dug in, my life began to change in extraordinary ways. The living power of God's Word began to transform me.

In Matthew 4:4, Jesus tells us that man shall not live by bread alone but by every word that comes from the mouth of God. We should regard the Bible as God's Word, as if he were directly speaking to us in the present tense. To fully understand the message, we may need to read and re-read the verses that speak to us. We may need a study guide or a commentary to help us understand the underlying meaning of each verse. But eventually, the words start to come to life. From God's Word, we will discover powerful lessons and principles that are intended to guide us in our daily lives. As you mature spiritually, you'll begin to notice that you can compare the truth from any teaching by comparing it with the teachings of the Bible. You can rely on the Bible as your most important, unequivocal, reliable source for the ultimate truth.

More than just hearing the Word of God, we must put this newly discovered truth into action. We can apply what we have learned to our daily experiences and encounters. If we miss the opportunity to put these teachings to work in our complicated lives, we may never experience God's complete plan for us. In James 1:22, we are reminded that we must be "doers" of the word and not just "hearers." We deceive ourselves when we don't take action. The more we invest ourselves in knowing God's Word, the more we open ourselves to the Spirit's voice, which empowers us to take action and grow as Christians. His word is sufficient for our every need. Trust it.

MY PRAYER

Father, God, let me immerse myself in the living power of your Word. Let me be transformed by the wisdom that comes directly from you. Give me the desire to hear the word and then apply it to serving you. For these things, we pray in the name of your son, Jesus. Amen.

READ: JAMES 1:21-25

QUESTION #1: How might you create the necessary margin in your life to devote more time to reading and understanding God's Word?

QUESTION #2: What steps can you take to encourage others to spend time in God's word?

CONTEMPLATE

Think about a time in your life when you found comfort or wisdom from reading the Bible. Describe the circumstances. How did this experience change your life?

SPIRITUAL WARFARE

For we wanted to come to you—certainly I, Paul, did, again and again—but Satan blocked our way. (1 Thessalonians 2:18)

I remember seeing cartoons when I was a little kid that depicted Satan as a pesky little guy in a red jumpsuit with horns, tail, and pitchfork sitting on the shoulder of a contemplative man who also had the stereotypical image of angel on the opposite shoulder. Most often, this person was wrestling with temptation and trying to decide between good and evil. Over time, the devil got lumped in with the make-believe status of monsters under the bed, the boogeyman, Sasquatch and the Loch Ness monster. The devil was so darn cute that my mother let me dress up like him for at least three or four consecutive Halloweens. Like so many others, we made a huge mistake by not taking Satan seriously. It would take me decades to realize that Satan was real and that he had my name on his list.

In Luke 10:17-20, we learn that God has delegated a degree of authority to Satan. Paul firmly believed that Satan was keeping him from returning to Thessalonica and that's why he dispatched Timothy to go on his behalf. The truth of the matter is that Satan is the temporary ruler of this world and he is constantly searching for ways to distract and separate us from God. That's one of the many reasons scripture frequently reminds us that we are not of this world. Our eternal home is with God, but until Jesus returns, the devil is going to have some power over our lives. His actions are one reason that so many of us struggle with complacency and failing to accomplish what God called us to do.

In James 4:7, we are told to submit to God and to resist Satan. A house divided cannot stand. God's hope is that the frustrations, setbacks, and distractions caused by the evil one will work for the benefit of our spiritual maturity. God wants us to be victorious over Satan and he knows that the more often we overcome the devil, the stronger and more effective we will be as Christians. In light of this, we can protect ourselves by first acknowledging that we are under attack and then submitting ourselves to God. This will help to minimize the yardage gained by spiritual warfare in our lives. Satan is powerful, but he can do nothing to us without our cooperation.

MY PRAYER

God, keep me ever mindful that Satan is plotting against me. The closer I get to you, the stronger his attacks will become. Make me resilient, steadfast and vigilant. Give me the courage to be victorious over Satan's power. We pray for these things in the name of your son, Jesus Christ. Amen.

READ: 2 CORINTHIANS 2:10-11

QUESTION #1: In what part of your day are you most susceptible to Satan's attacks?

QUESTION #2: In what ways do you believe Satan is plotting against you right now?

CONTEMPLATE

Recall a season in your life when you believe you might have been under attack by Satan. What were the circumstances? How might the outcome have been different if you were aware that you were under attack? How did you fail to stand firm? How did you resist?

YOUR SPIRITUAL RESUME

For what is our hope, our joy, or the crown in which we will glory in the presence of our Lord Jesus when he comes? Is it not you? Indeed, you are our glory and joy. (1 Thessalonians 2:19-20)

For much of our adult lives, we spend a disproportionate amount of time thinking about our professional accomplishments and how we can strategically climb the corporate ladder or gain status. When all is said and done, our value in heaven won't have much to do with whether our resume is one page or 14 pages. Instead, we are more likely to be measured by the number of people we brought closer to Christ. It's an unconventional way to keep score by earthly standards, but Paul reminds us that there is no greater joy than to know you brought someone else to Christ.

We recruit teams for golf tournaments, softball leagues and even for a bowling night. In our more noble endeavors, sometimes we recruit teams for charity events, walkathons, and fundraising drives. But what about God's team? How successful have we been in recruiting our colleagues, neighbors, relatives, and customers to know God? What is it that makes us feel completely comfortable to ask a friend to invest in a questionable network marketing scheme, but yet it is outside our comfort zone to invite them to church, a Bible study or for a cup of coffee where you can share the story of your journey towards a personal relationship with Christ?

In a like manner, our culture makes it perfectly acceptable to mentor a young man in the business world, imparting our wisdom and advice on how he could be more successful, productive and valuable in his profession. So why is there a social stigma associated with offering the sage advice that will give him an eternal life and happiness? The answer is that our priorities are completely out of order. When you meet Christ, do you think the entire focus is going to be just on the good things you have done in your life or how many times you went to church? Wouldn't you like to look around and see all of your friends and family members standing there with you? It's time to start building a resume that has a real mission statement. No references required. God already knows.

MY PRAYER

Father, God, let me be the coach, quarterback, and cheerleader dedicated to building a team of believers destined for heaven. Let me dedicate myself to being mindful of your call for me to be a fisher of men. Let my worth in your kingdom be measured by the team I have built in your honor. I pray for these things in the name of your son, Jesus Christ. Amen.

READ: ACTS 26:14-18

QUESTION #1: Who are the people you should be recruiting for God's team? Make a list of the five people who should be on your heart for Christ.

QUESTION #2: What are the obstacles that keep you from talking about your faith with those people?

CONTEMPLATE

Recall the conversation with the first person who talked to you about a relationship with Christ. Was it a parent, friend or complete stranger? How did that conversation make you feel?

PUSHING THROUGH THE PAIN

In fact, when we were with you, we kept telling you that we would be persecuted. And it turned out that way, as you well know. For this reason, when I could stand it no longer, I sent to find out about your faith. I was afraid that in some way the tempter had tempted you and that our labors might have been in vain. (1 Thessalonians 3:4-5)

Have you ever wanted something so bad that you were actually willing to endure pain for it? Maybe you've trained for a marathon? Maybe you wanted to serve in the military and knew that you had to endure basic training before you could be called a soldier? Maybe you've suffered through withdrawal and detoxification while trying to overcome an addiction? It's easier to endure suffering when you know there's a reward waiting for you. But what about the suffering that comes from losing a loved one, fighting an aggressive cancer, or facing persecution like the Thessalonians?

God wants us to know there's a reward for that kind of suffering as well.

Grace can be described as God's power in us to do the things we could not do under our own power. In 2 Corinthians 12:9-10, Jesus tells us that His grace is sufficient for us and that His strength is perfected in our weakness. When we are weak, God is strong. His power strengthens us and allows us to triumph over evil. Through this process, our character is strengthened and we are better prepared to weather the next storm. It is all part of a process that builds endurance, stability, and wisdom. Once we've built our house on a strong foundation, very little can be done to destroy it. In life's deepest valleys, we should find comfort in knowing that God is with us along the way. He doesn't always take away our problems, but he always sees us through them.

Paul tells us our troubles are the work of Satan. In Ephesians 6:10-18, he shares how we can protect ourselves from demonic threats: put on the full Armor of God. We are safe from the enemy when we allow our truth, righteousness, peace, faith and the Holy Spirit to defend us. In the midst of the enemy's attacks, be encouraged by the knowledge that God is with you at all times. There is a reward waiting at the end of the battle.

MY PRAYER

God, let me begin each day knowing that You are with me through every challenge. Let my exasperation turn to joy knowing that good things await me at the end of each and every trial. Let me focus on the hope instead of the pain. For these things, we pray in the name of your son, Jesus Christ. Amen.

READ: 2 CORINTHIANS 12:7-10

QUESTION #1: What circumstance in your life is causing the greatest pain and suffering right now?

QUESTION #2: What reward might be waiting for you at the end of this season of suffering?

CONTEMPLATE

Write about an event in your life that was painful and difficult to endure at the time but now you recognize as something that helped make you stronger. Try to describe your feelings at the time and compare them to how you now feel.

STANDING FIRM

Therefore, brothers and sisters, in all our distress and persecution we were encouraged about you because of your faith. For now we really live, since you are standing firm in the Lord. (1 Thessalonians 3:7-8)

Paul was elated when he received word back from Timothy that the new believers in Thessalonica—in spite of the persecution they were enduring—were standing firm in their faith. Paul himself had experienced so much suffering and retribution for spreading God's Word that he was deeply concerned that those who were immature in their faith would not be willing to withstand the abuse. The example Paul set for others was a powerful motivator to stay true to the cause. Like a good leader, he modeled the type of self-sacrifice that would be necessary to advance God's kingdom. He had no ulterior motives in doing so, and the new believers in Thessalonica knew it.

Today, nearly one-third of the world's population are Christians. With 2.1 billion fellow believers, there are few parts of the world where Christians face the obstacles that Paul faced. In addition to what has happened in recent years in the Islamic State, Christians have also been persecuted in Africa, throughout the Middle East, and within China. Those of us living in Western Civilization have little to fear by standing firm in our faith. Even so, in our modern culture, men still struggle to stand up for what they believe, especially when it comes to their faith. As Christians, our core beliefs are tied to the virtues of prudence, justice, temperance, and courage. However, in the company of other men, we often fail to demonstrate those values. Regrettably, we are more likely to stand up and defend our country or favorite sports team than to stand up and defend our religious beliefs.

The writings of the Apostle Paul remind us to live lives that are worthy of the Gospel and to stand firm in our faith so that others will see the benefits that come with being a member of God's family. This type of steadfast courage is especially important to new believers who have not yet experienced the work of God in all of its splendor. Once they've developed the necessary discipline, they, too, will flourish as a child of God and become a light for others to see. In a like manner, we must use our faith to encourage others, building them up to become outstanding citizens of the Kingdom of God.

MY PRAYER

Father, God, let me set an example for others in how I live my life. Let me be mindful of the needs of new believers who are still finding their way toward you. God, give me strength, especially in the presence of other men, to stand by my values and be true to the virtues of my faith. For these things, I pray in the name of your son, Jesus Christ. Amen.

READ: PHILIPPIANS 1:27–30

QUESTION #1: What prevents you from standing firm in your faith while in the presence of others?

QUESTION #2: How might you modify your behavior in the presence of other men to demonstrate the benefits of living a Christian life?

CONTEMPLATE

Write about a time when you encountered someone whose behavior did not match the Christian image they claimed. How did their actions contradict their Christian beliefs? How did your opinion of them change as a result of that experience?

"May the Lord make your love increase and overflow for each other and for everyone else, just as ours does for you. May he strengthen your hearts so that you will be blameless and holy in the presence of our God and Father when our Lord Jesus comes with all his holy ones."

(1 Thessalonians 3:12)

WEEK 3

SHOWING GRATITUDE

How can we thank God enough for you in return for all the joy we have in the presence of our God because of you? Night and day we pray most earnestly that we may see you again and supply what is lacking in your faith. (1 Thessalonians 3:9-10)

Paul was overjoyed by the fact that so many Thessalonians had continued to pursue God and had stayed true to their spiritual endeavors. Paul considered it a blessing in his life that God had put the Thessalonians in his life. It might have been tempting for Paul to pat himself on the back for his accomplishments on behalf of God's kingdom, but he knew better. Paul knew the credit belonged to God. God did the most important work. He simply used Paul as a medium to accomplish his goals. As prospective disciples, we can take comfort in knowing that God is doing the heavy lifting by preparing the hearts of the men and women we will eventually bring to Christ.

Just as the Thessalonians were grateful for Paul sharing the good news of God, we too should be thankful for those who took the time and effort to bring us to Christ. Whether it was a parent, coach, Sunday school teacher, or a friend from work, they deserve our utmost gratitude. The man who challenged me to pursue a personal relationship with Christ did not know me well at the time, but he took the risk of reaching out to me and inviting me to hear his story. We met at his office and he opened the Bible and asked me to read from five different passages. That experience was a new beginning for me. I felt loved and valued, not only by this man but also by God. The weeks and months that followed were life-changing. I eventually gained the confidence and strong sense of responsibility that I needed to pay it forward with other men. God made all of it possible in a way that only God, himself, could orchestrate. I may have been among the least likely of people God would use for this purpose.

If you remember the person who first brought you to Christ, take a moment to reach out to them to thank them for the important role he or she played in your spiritual journey. If that person has passed on, take a moment to thank God for putting that person in your life. Psalm 136:1 reminds us to give our thanks to the Lord because he is good and his love endures forever. Showing gratitude for all things great or small is the sign of a mature Christian who has learned to recognize the blessings that fill our complicated lives.

MY PRAYER

God, help me to make gratitude an integral part of my daily life. Teach me to be thankful for the things I take for granted. Let me show my appreciation for all things. God, I ask today for your special blessings for those who labored to bring me closer to you. I pray for these things in the name of your son, Jesus Christ. Amen.

READ: PSALM 30:1-12

QUESTION #1: Who was the person who first approached you about the benefits of living a life committed to God? What was your reaction to the invitation?

QUESTION #2: Do you feel compelled to invite someone to explore a personal relationship with Christ right now? If so, write their name(s) in the margin of this page.

CONTEMPLATE

What were the circumstances that led you to Christ? What do you recall about the initial invitation? Describe the details.

ALL YOU NEED IS LOVE

May the Lord make your love increase and overflow for each other and for everyone else, just as ours does for you. May he strengthen your hearts so that you will be blameless and holy in the presence of our God and Father when our Lord Jesus comes with all his holy ones. (1 Thessalonians 3:12)

You may recall the story from Matthew 22 where the Pharisees pressed Jesus to identify the most important of the Commandments. Jesus replied: "Love the Lord your God with all your heart and with all your soul and with all your mind." This is the first and greatest commandment. And the second is like it: "Love your neighbor as yourself." Even if you're someone who struggles to understand much of what is written in the Bible, Jesus could not have put the importance of love in any simpler terms. In his letter to Thessalonica, Paul drove home the same message. Paul made known his love for his readers and asked that they do the same for each other.

Love can do amazing things and, through it, all things are possible. However, sometimes it's admittedly difficult to love those who seem unlovable. In the context of our daily lives, we encounter some pretty undesirable characters along the way. Frankly, it's easy to love people who are like us. Those who share similar socio-economic traits or interests or those who look and think like us. But what about those who have different belief systems, accents, or lifestyles? What about those who we believe are living disgraceful lives? Do we love them as we should?

In 1 Peter 4:8, we learn that above all things, we are to have fervent love for one another. Even better, we are told that love will cover a multitude of sins. The message is clear. We are to love our enemies and bless those who curse us. Perhaps the most difficult of all, we are to pray for those who persecute us. No matter how good of a Christian you may be, that's a tall order. Extending our love to the unlovable is a way of honoring a God who steadfastly loves each and every one of us, regardless of our warts, indiscretions, and repeated failures. Do you love others despite their failures, indiscretions, and shortcomings? Or is your love contingent on their moral probity and social fitness? Paul's love for the Thessalonians was a reflection of God's unqualified love; make your love for others the same.

MY PRAYER

God, let love be my first and last resort as I encounter others along the path of my journey. Let me put as much of my heart into loving those who are different as I put into those who are like me. Let me love unconditionally, in all circumstances, every day of my life. I pray for these things in the name of your son, Jesus Christ. Amen.

READ: MATTHEW 5:43-45

QUESTION #1: Name a person you know who is difficult for you to love. Can you imagine finding it in your heart to love this person?

QUESTION #2: What makes you difficult to love? How did Jesus treat you despite those things?

CONTEMPLATE

Write a letter to someone whom you find difficult to love. Ask for forgiveness and ask to help you mend the difficult relationship you have with him or her.

SEXUAL SIN

It is God's will that you should be sanctified: that you should avoid sexual immorality; that each of you should learn to control your own body in a way that is holy and honorable, not in passionate lust like the pagans, who do not know God; and that in this matter no one should wrong or take advantage of a brother or sister. The Lord will punish all those who commit such sins, as we told you and warned you before. For God did not call us to be impure, but to live a holy life. Therefore, anyone who rejects this instruction does not reject a human being but God, the very God who gives you his Holy Spirit. (1 Thessalonians 4:1-8)

M en have struggled with sexual purity for thousands of years. Some will claim that a man's sexual appetite is built into his DNA and is somehow tied to our primal desires to hunt, gather and procreate. If that were true, it wouldn't be a sin. Man's problem with lust is a problem of the heart. Paul knew that his new believers in Thessalonica would be tempted by the robust sexual activity that was part of the Roman Empire. In those times, it was common for a man to have a wife for having children and a mistress on the side for recreational activity. Paul used this letter to tell men to focus on getting their sexual appetites under control. As odd as it may seem, sex with prostitutes at the local temple was not considered a vice, but a moral duty. This was a radical idea of this culture. While women were expected to be chaste and keep sex within the confines of marriage, men were not.

The good news for Christian men is that sex, in itself, is NOT a sin. In Corinthians 7:1-9, we learn that God created sex for all of his creatures to enjoy. However, sex outside the parameters of marriage is a sin. Any form of adultery, premarital or extramarital sex is immoral. Looking at pornography or having lustful thoughts for someone other than your wife is also sinful. Sexual sin separates us from God and drives a wedge into our most intimate relationships with our loved ones. A man addicted to pornography is likely to also struggle with anger, compulsivity, shame, drug abuse and intimacy.

The battle with sexual sin and lust begins in the mind. You've heard the phrase, "Garbage in, garbage out." When you view pornography or let your eyes wander along the curvaceous form of an attractive woman who is not your wife, you are essentially allowing lust to stir up passions and emotions that expand our capacity for sin. If we are weak, we lose our inhibitions and our desires blast through any shred of willpower we once had to stay morally upright. The consequences of our sexual sin are devastating, both physically and spiritually. While Jesus forgives us for our sexual sin, it's likely that those impacted most by your indiscretions will be less likely to extend that kind of grace.

MY PRAYER

God, give me the discipline I need to avoid the temptation and lustful thoughts that lead to sexual sin. Instead, let my focus be on the relationship that I have with you. Let all of my thoughts and activities be only those which honor you. For these things, I pray in the name of your son, Jesus Christ. Amen.

READ: 2 TIMOTHY :22

QUESTION #1: Under what circumstances do you tend to struggle with sexual impurity?

QUESTION #2: What steps can you take to avoid those circumstances?

CONTEMPLATE

Write a letter to yourself when you were 12 years old. What advice would you have given yourself about the complexities of sexual sin? What steps could you have taken to maintain purity in your life? What advice would you offer regarding the temptation to view pornography?

FINDING PURPOSE

...and to make it your ambition to lead a quiet life: You should mind your own business and work with your hands, just as we told you, so that your daily life may win the respect of outsiders and so that you will not be dependent on anybody. (1 Thessalonians 4:11-12)

When some of the Thessalonians learned from Paul's teachings that Christ would be returning one day, they immediately stopped working and began to prepare for his triumphant return. For some, this knowledge became part of a convenient excuse as many Greeks looked down on manual labor to begin with. This concerned Paul because he knew that his new believers who continued working would soon begin to resent those who did not. Paul also knew that idle hands were the devil's workshop. In addition to losing the respect of those around them, these loafers would soon be getting themselves into trouble. Paul encouraged all of his new believers to find a purpose and stay focused because an honest day's work was a powerful testimony and influence on those who did not have Christ in their lives.

All of us need a sense of purpose in our work. If you feel stuck or you've simply noticed that you don't have much joy in your labors, it's time to turn to God to find the answers that will give your life a sense of direction, and more importantly, a sense of purpose. In Psalms 57:2, David sings, "I cry out to God Most High, to God who fulfills his purpose for me." All of us know people who are passionate about their relationships and the people with whom they are engaged. Wondering why others have more rewarding and meaningful work is common, especially if our relationship with God is incomplete.

What about the value of our work on behalf of the kingdom? We aren't like the Greeks who disdained labor, or aristocrats who extracted wealth for laborers. Instead, we understand that while work has been cursed by human sin, it is still good. In the resurrection, we will not cease working, we will simply do it with joy unto the glory of God. So the best way to prepare for Jesus's return is not laying down the hammer, it's swinging it joyfully for the glory of God and for the sake of his kingdom on earth as in heaven.

MY PRAYER

God, give me the wisdom to recognize my strengths and talents so that I may serve you with a purpose and a passion that is contagious. Let me help others recognize their gifts for a strong sense of purpose and a desire to build a relationship with you. May you be glorified in all that I do with my gifts. I pray for these things in the name of your son, Jesus Christ. Amen.

READ: JEREMIAH 29:11-14

QUESTION #1: In what ways do you find purpose in your work?

QUESTION #2: Do you feel passionate about this purpose? Why or why not?

CONTEMPLATE

Ask a trusted friend to help you make a list of your strengths and gifts. Next, make a list of the things you are most passionate about. How do these two lists compare with one another? Is there a common ground or theme? Write a short prayer asking God for clarity in discovering your true purpose.

BLESSED ASSURANCE

According to the Lord's word, we tell you that we who are still alive, who are left until the coming of the Lord, will certainly not precede those who have fallen asleep. For the Lord, himself will come down from heaven, with a loud command, with the voice of the archangel and with the trumpet call of God, and the dead in Christ will rise first. After that, we who are still alive and are left will be caught up together with them in the clouds to meet the Lord in the air. And so we will be with the Lord forever. Therefore encourage one another with these words. (1 Thessalonians 4:15-18)

The Thessalonians were anxiously anticipating the return of Christ and became frustrated when they lost loved ones, fearing that death would prevent them from joining their loved ones in heaven once Christ returned. Paul had to give these new believers assurance that Christ would raise all who believed in him, both the living and the dead. The gift of salvation was as hard to comprehend back then as it is today. In a skeptical and cynical world, Christ's promise to us seems too good to be true. When we die, our souls will go to heaven and our bodies will remain on this earth until the rapture when our bodies will be resurrected and transformed just as Christ's body was resurrected. This may conflict with your view of the rapture…and that's okay. Be sure to read my friend Patrick Miller's essay on this complicated topic on pages 97 to 101 of this book.

For some, this promise requires a deep level of faith. Having the full assurance of faith requires patience much like a newly planted seed. It is a delicate process that takes time and requires a significant amount of nurturing. Like the germinating seed, our confidence is fragile at first, but the deeper the roots grow and the more time that passes, our confidence grows and we begin to understand that God's Word may be the only real truth in our lives. God's method of nurturing us may involve seeing us through trials and hardships along the way so that our faith can be matured and strengthened. When our faith is proven, we become more steadfast and resilient to the things that might have once wiped us out. Assurance is one of the many benefits that come out of our growing relationship with God.

One way we strengthen our sense of assurance is by leaning into our hope. For Christians, our ultimate hope is not to escape from this world, but to see it renewed under the lordship of Christ. We know that when he returns our bodies will be resurrected, and we will know death no more. This world, as well, will be transformed, so that the curse of sin and death have no hold over it. Instead, we will build an eternal civilization for his glory, enjoying his creation as faithful laborers.

MY PRAYER

God, give me the courage to share the story of your promises with anyone who has doubts about the goodness of our Lord. Let me encourage and reassure new believers of the good things that are to come in their relationship with you. I pray for these things in the name of your son, Jesus Christ. Amen.

READ: JOHN 14:1-3

QUESTION #1: What steps can you take to give new believers increased confidence in God's assurances?

QUESTION #2: At what point in your life was your faith tested? What was the outcome?

CONTEMPLATE

Write about your experiences as a Christian that have reassured you in the goodness of God's promises in your life. Be specific. What do you believe led you to these experiences?

*"Therefore encourage one another and
build each other up, just as in fact you are doing."*

(1 Thessalonians 5:11)

WEEK 4

ENCOURAGE ONE ANOTHER

For God did not appoint us to suffer wrath but to receive salvation through our Lord Jesus Christ. He died for us so that, whether we are awake or asleep, we may live together with him. Therefore encourage one another and build each other up, just as in fact you are doing. (1 Thessalonians 5:9-11)

Perhaps you've heard the saying, "Every man needs a Paul, Barnabas, and Timothy in his life." We know that Paul was a mentor to many. We also know that Timothy was someone who benefited greatly from Paul's mentoring. But who was Barnabas? You can read about Barnabas in Acts 4 and Acts 14. He was one of the apostles of the early church who traveled with Paul on missionary trips. We know that he was a tireless worker and was very generous in his financial support of the early church. But more importantly, Barnabas was someone who was known as a great encourager. In fact, Barnabas wasn't his birth name. It was a nickname given to him by his fellow apostles, which translates into English as "Son of Encouragement."

Christ calls upon us to be responsive to the needs of others. We all know what it's like to have a discouraging day or to go through a challenging season in our life. Not only does God call us to encourage one another, but he wants us to do it frequently. In Hebrews 3:13, we read, "But encourage one another daily, as long as it is called "Today," so that none of you may be hardened by sin's deceitfulness." We are called to be our brother's keeper and we should take that responsibility seriously. More than just tending to his physical and emotional needs, we must also take great concern over his spiritual needs. We need to take a personal interest in his walk and help him make good choices. The best kind of encouragement we can give another person is to help him connect with Christ.

How can we encourage others? It starts by knowing that words really matter. Ephesians 4:29 reminds us that the only words that should come out of our mouths are those that build up other people. When we encourage one another, our ultimate hope is that our words will lift someone's heart towards God. When someone comes to us with a problem, we can respond to their circumstances with empathy but we should also go that extra step and offer up a sense of hope and encouragement. We can give them a fresh perspective and help them envision a positive resolution to their concerns. Our words of encouragement should be specific and genuine, otherwise, they will ring hollow. Encouraging others must be a part of our daily routine.

MY PRAYER

God, let me be inspired by the example of Barnabas and become a "Son of Encouragement" to those around me. Help me to be responsive when someone needs a kind word or a gesture of reassurance. I pray for these things in the name of your son, Jesus. Amen.

READ: EPHESIANS 4:29-32

QUESTION #1: Recall a time when someone changed your life with his or her words of encouragement. How did that experience affect you?

QUESTION #2: Would people in your office call you a "son of encouragement?

CONTEMPLATE

Write about the way you recognize the achievements of others at meetings. Do you enjoy giving credit to others and lifting them up in the presence of your superiors?

LONELY AT THE TOP

Now we ask you, brothers and sisters, to acknowledge those who work hard among you, who care for you in the Lord and who admonish you. Hold them in the highest regard in love because of their work. Live in peace with each other. (1 Thessalonians 5:12-13)

E very year, I host a Christian men's conference where we bring in some of the nation's most influential pastors on topics of spiritual importance to men. A couple of years ago, I came across a young pastor who had written a couple of thought-provoking books and, by all accounts, was well on his way to becoming one of the rising stars in Christian ministry. In spite of his incredible talent, energy, and enthusiasm for God's Word, he committed suicide a few months after speaking at our conference. He left behind a beautiful wife, two young children and a burgeoning ministry that held great promise. In the end, the pressures associated with building his church and finding some sense of balance became too overwhelming.

Tragically, countless high-profile pastors have fallen in the last decade. But it's not just celebrity pastors who are disappearing. A recent Barna study showed that 38% of pastors considered quitting ministry in 2021 alone. The pressures of political polarization, the pandemic, and an overall decrease in congregational mental health have crushed everyday church leaders. They feel alone and exhausted by the critiques and cynicism.

When you think about it, there's much more to a pastor's life than what you witness during a one-hour service on Sunday mornings.

Shepherding a flock gives you exposure to the best and worst of humanity. Imagine being the trusted person to whom countless people confess their sorrows, sins, infidelities, addictions, insecurities, and moral weaknesses. Pastors tend to be the refuge we seek when life's challenges are too overwhelming. Paul derived so much satisfaction in the good news that Timothy and Silas brought from Thessalonica that it gave new energy to his ministry. His advice to his new believers was to encourage and nurture their pastors. What can you do to lift your pastor's burdens? What can you do to feed or nourish their souls?

MY PRAYER

Father, God, let me be intentional in my efforts to encourage those who lead your church. Let me be the one who feeds the good shepherd with praise and thanksgiving. Show me where I can be of assistance and where I can lift the burden of those who serve in such a noble way. Amen.

READ: HEBREWS 13:17-18

QUESTION #1: Describe the pastor who has had the greatest impact on your life. What are the things that likely sustained that pastor through good times and bad?

QUESTION #2: Think of a way that you can praise your pastor the next time you see him. What specific thing will you help him celebrate?

CONTEMPLATE

Make a list of the ways in which you can lighten the burden for the pastor of your church. In what ways can you rejuvenate and restore his passion for serving others?

REJOICE ALWAYS

Rejoice always, pray continually, give thanks in all circumstances; for this is God's will for you in Christ Jesus. (1 Thessalonians 5:16-18)

T he next time someone challenges you to memorize a Bible verse, you'll want to quickly revert back to 1 Thessalonians 5:16 which simply reads, "Rejoice always." It's more than just an easy verse to memorize. It's a verse that is packed with so much meaning and, quite possibly, the one verse in the Bible that could lead you to happiness for the rest of your life. Paul's message to the Thessalonians was intended to encourage them during prolonged stands of persecution. He longed for them to find the kind of joy that transcends even the most trying of circumstances. Paul wanted them to understand that their demeanor should not be connected to the events of the day or how things might be going in their lives. Instead, he wanted them to focus on the joy that emanates from having a unique relationship with God.

The best way to bring about joy is to practice thanksgiving in all that we do. Focusing on our many blessings and the abundance of things for which we have to be thankful can take the sting out of the unpleasant seasons of our lives. If this seems difficult, I would encourage you to create a Gratitude Journal. Use this journal to write down all of the things for which you are thankful, especially those things you most often take for granted. I often begin with thanksgiving for my family, my church, my community, my friends, my career, and the things in nature that only God could be responsible for.

Over the course of time, I am reminded of something in my life for which I should be thankful. When possible, I stop what I'm doing and go to my journal to add that new item to my list. At the same time, I admonish myself for only occasionally remembering those things for which I should be grateful. Paul wants us to live each moment of our lives in an ongoing state of thanksgiving and joy for both our blessings and the unique relationship we have with God. God's goodness never fades and we should commit ourselves to focus on the good in our lives rather than dwelling on the temporary challenges of this temporary life.

MY PRAYER

Father, God, you are so good. Lead me to a deeper understanding of the depth of your goodness and the joy that you want me to experience in this life and beyond. Fill me with thanksgiving and gratitude for every moment regardless of the circumstances. I pray for these things in the name of your son, Jesus. Amen.

READ: PHILIPPIANS 4:4-7

QUESTION #1: What do you think characterizes your life more right now: gratitude or dissatisfaction? What can you do to change your outlook?

QUESTION #2: Make a list of things you are thankful for today.

CONTEMPLATE

Create a plan to show thankfulness every day so that you can rejoice in God's goodness throughout the day.

PRAY CONTINUALLY

Rejoice always, pray continually, give thanks in all circumstances; for this is God's will for you in Christ Jesus. (1 Thessalonians 5:16-18)

What does it mean to pray continually? Is that even possible? Even with his own proclivity for prayer, it wasn't Paul's intention that we be in a constant state of prayer. Instead, Paul was encouraging persistence in prayer that would allow us to be constantly in communion with God. Paul wanted our first instinct to be to go to prayer in any circumstance. When you encounter an unexpected setback, go to God in prayer. When you receive good news, go to God in prayer. When you're frustrated or disappointed, go to God in prayer. Praying continually is more about making God the focal point of your daily life. It's about strengthening a prayer reflex in all circumstances.

For some, the definition of praying without ceasing means to develop a sense of dependence on God that is as innate as if we each had a hard-wired connection to God. The choices we make and the thoughts we have are driven by our desire to live a life that pleases God. In Colossians 4, we are reminded to be vigilant in our prayer life and to pray earnestly in a spirit of thanksgiving. We know that the joy we experience is driven by our ability to be thankful for all circumstances in our lives, both good and difficult. For that reason, we should be constantly mindful of the things for which we should have gratitude. If you think you've run out of things to pray about, start with those things for which you are grateful.

Our prayer life should permeate all that we do. If you're someone who's not in the habit of praying at dinner or at night before you go to sleep, being in a state of constant prayer may sound like an unreasonable expectation. Start by taking baby steps in your prayer life. It takes several days of repetition to create a habit but there are ways to become intentional about praying. You could start by praying while you brush your teeth or while you're driving to work. I have found that praying right before I fall asleep gives me a chance to reflect on my day and evaluate whether or not I'm living a life that pleases God. On most occasions, I realize that I'm falling short of being the man that God intends so that gives me a chance to seek his forgiveness and create a plan to do better tomorrow. If you want to increase your confidence in the power of prayer, read Mark 11:24, "Therefore I tell you, whatever you ask for in prayer, believe that you have received it, and it will be yours."

MY PRAYER

God, teach me to pray. Let me put my complete trust in you so that I can find myself in communion with you through every part of my day. Let me rejoice and give thanks in my relationship with you. I pray for these things in the name of your son, Jesus Christ. Amen.

READ: LUKE 11:1-13

QUESTION #1: How would your life be different if you had the discipline to be in a persistent state of prayer?

QUESTION #2: What keeps you from praying more often?

CONTEMPLATE

Create a plan to start praying more frequently. Don't be overly ambitious. Start with small, actionable items.

GIVE THANKS

Rejoice always, pray continually, give thanks in all circumstances; for this is God's will for you in Christ Jesus. (1 Thessalonians 5:16-18)

P erhaps you're familiar with the adage, "Keep your eyes on the prize." Not only is the phrase commonly used to encourage people who experience temporary setbacks, it was also the name of a folk song that was made popular during the civil rights movement in America. The message is still relevant today, especially when we think of it in the context of our spiritual journeys. No matter what happens in our lives, if we stay focused on the future joy we will experience with Christ, the little bumps along the roads of life are but a small distraction. If you believe that God creates a purpose in every circumstance, then it makes sense that you embrace the belief that we should be giving thanks not only for our prosperity but also for the adversity that comes our way.

In Romans 8:28, we are reminded that "in all things, God works for the good of those who love him, who have been called according to his purpose." We may not be thankful for the diagnosis of cancer; however, we can be thankful that our God is a healer and has the power to cure us of cancer. We aren't thankful for persecution, but thankful that we have a God who will lead us through the persecution. When we encounter challenging times, our thankfulness will keep us connected to Jesus. Even if our hardships end in death, or losing someone we love, we know that our God is the resurrector, who will make all things new. Sometimes, it takes looking in the rearview mirror to completely understand God's complicated and perfect plan for our lives.

Being thankful in the difficult times was Paul's message to the Thessalonians in the midst of their many trials. Paul encouraged these new believers to lean into their faith, adopting a mindset of thanksgiving, even when they felt like they were entitled to feelings of deep disappointment. Today's troubles are tomorrow's victories. God's promises are better than gold. When you feel overwhelmed by your worldly challenges, turn to Psalm 23 and be reminded that God walks with us through the valleys in our life and he gives us hope in our losses and joy in our sorrows. He also gives us encouragement and love when we experience disappointment. How much more assurance do we need than that?

MY PRAYER

God, give me the discipline to live with a continual spirit of thanksgiving through all of the circumstances in my life, no matter how challenging they may seem. Let me focus on the future joy that I will have in your presence through eternity. I pray for these things in the name of your son, Jesus. Amen.

READ: ROMANS 8:28-30

QUESTION #1: What causes you to lose sight of your ultimate prize in Christ: resurrection with him?

QUESTION #2: How have you seen God guide you in your darkest moments?

CONTEMPLATE

Write about a situation or event that you once perceived as a setback that turned out to be a blessing. What changed your perspective? How can you apply this lesson to future setbacks?

"May God himself, the God of peace, sanctify you through and through. May your whole spirit, soul and body be kept blameless at the coming of our Lord Jesus Christ."

(1 Thessalonians 5:23)

WEEK 5

TRUST, BUT VERIFY!

Do not quench the Spirit. Do not treat prophecies with contempt but test them all; hold on to what is good, reject every kind of evil. (1 Thessalonians 5:19-22)

Have you ever had a friend or acquaintance tell you that God told them to do something? Maybe God told them to quit their job or to give away all of their money? In complete transparency, my first response to a comment like this is usually one of doubt. To the best of my knowledge, God has never directly told me to do anything. I have tried sitting in silence for hours. I've attempted to calm my mind so that if God has something to say to me, I am ready to hear it. There have been multiple times in my life where I would have given anything to have had God tell me what to do. Far too often, "prophets" give words to people that end up wrecking their lives. They claim to speak with God's voice, but, in the end, it's just the delusions of an arrogant human.

In 1 Corinthians 12:1-11, we learn that the gifts of the Holy Spirit are wisdom, understanding, counsel, fortitude, knowledge, piety, and an appropriate fear of the Lord. If we allow the Holy Spirit to do its work in our lives, we will inadvertently submit to God's will in our lives. Paul warns the Thessalonians to be aware of false prophets who may be trying to sway them in the wrong direction. He further encourages them to be respectful of church leaders, treating them with respect but with a caveat to test them against the truth of scripture. A common theme in Thessalonians repeated frequently by Paul is to trust and encourage church leadership, but use discernment to verify that their teachings are in line with God's Word.

In 1 Corinthians 14, Paul warns that these gifts of the Holy Spirit should be used to encourage, comfort, and strengthen others. However, Paul also reminds us that virtue (love) is greater than any of these gifts. If you don't have love, what good are the other gifts? While it is a blessing, it carries with it a tremendous burden of responsibility. Open your heart and mind to the possibility of receiving the gifts of the Holy Spirit. More importantly, make the decision to use these gifts with the love that God intended.

MY PRAYER

Heavenly Father, give me the love I need to receive the gifts of the Holy Spirit and give me the gift of discernment to recognize the gifts you've already given to me. Let me use these gifts to serve you by loving others. Amen.

READ: 1 CORINTHIANS 14

QUESTION #1: Have you ever had a spiritual prompting but chose not to act on it? Describe.

QUESTION #2: What steps can you take to refine your spiritual discernment to become more in tune with what the Holy Spirit wants to do in your life?

CONTEMPLATE

Make a list of the gifts of the Holy Spirit and how you could use these gifts to serve God. Which of these gifts do you desire most? Why?

LIVING AUTHENTICALLY

May God himself, the God of peace, sanctify you through and through.
May your whole spirit, soul and body be kept blameless at the coming of
our Lord Jesus Christ. The one who calls you is faithful, and he will do it.
(1 Thessalonians 5:23-24)

Men tend to live compartmentalized lives. Like a well-organized toolbox, there's a specific place for absolutely everything in our lives. We have our work life, which goes into one part of the box. We have our home life that goes into another part of the box. And there's that secret compartment of the box that contains the part of our life that even our best friends don't know about. Deep down inside we believe our lives will be easier to manage if we can keep the complicated relationships, emotions, and frustrations of one aspect of our lives separate from the others. But what about the box that nobody knows about? The one that's hidden in the bathroom closet or stuffed between the mattress? The things that tend to pull us into isolation are almost always the things that get us into the most trouble.

Few of us are the same guy at church as we are on the basketball court or in the locker room. One of our biggest struggles as Christians is maintaining some level of consistency in every aspect of our lives. Unfortunately, God is not interested in having a relationship with just the part of us sitting in that pew on Sunday morning, He wants all of us. For better or worse, God wants us to include him in every aspect of our lives. He wants us to live lives that truly reflect our relationship with him.

There are many downsides to living compartmentalized lives. The biggest negative is that, at times, we aren't emotionally available to those we love most. Secondly, there's a massive void of accountability when we keep everything neatly separated. To live a joyful life, we need to keep God in his rightful place and make him our first priority. God doesn't want us to live fractured lives. He wants us to live as whole men, whose personalities are fully integrated in the light. We need to start our day with God and get into his word to set the tone for the rest of the day. The best advice I've ever heard is to "make sure you let the WORD in before you let the WORLD in." To live authentically, we must remain teachable, put others first, allow our minds and emotions to be constantly renewed by the spirit, and align our actions and thoughts with what God is teaching us in the Word.

MY PRAYER

Father, God, give me the courage to let You into every aspect of my life. Let me live a life that is transparent and worthy of the gifts you have given me. Let me serve you on Sunday morning just as I serve you every other day of the week. For these things, I pray in the name of your son, Jesus Christ. Amen.

READ: MARK 12:29-30

QUESTION #1: What part of your current life are you most uncomfortable sharing with others?

QUESTION #2: What part of your life would you like to be delivered from?

CONTEMPLATE

Make a list of the things that you could change about your life to live a more consistent life in Christ. Rate each item on the list on a scale of 1 (easiest to change) to 10 (most difficult to change).

TRUST GOD'S TIMING

Therefore, among God's churches we boast about your perseverance and faith in all the persecutions and trials you are enduring. (2 Thessalonians 1:4)

Thanks to modern technology and innovation, we are largely living in an era of instant gratification. Beyond the benefits of instant rice and noodles and online shopping, we have become fixated on wanting the "good life" and wanting it NOW! When we are told that we might have to wait a few days or weeks to get something we want, we immediately start looking for someone else who can immediately give us what we need. I suppose that's part of the reason why so many of us struggle with the concept of accepting God's timing in our lives. Even if your faith is strong enough to believe that God will provide exactly what you need, you still have that burning question: "Why is it taking so long?"

The Thessalonians were wondering how much longer they would have to endure the persecution and abuse they were facing. Paul had promised that God would reward them for being steadfast but he could not give them a set timeline for God's triumphant return or when their trials would subside. They were beginning to question whether or not that day would ever come. Paul reassured them that their perseverance would not go unnoticed. We all have a lot to learn about tenacity under duress. Most of us will never face the kind of persecution experienced by the Thessalonians. Our Christian journeys would be dramatically enhanced if we could learn to become more patient as we grow deeper in our faith.

In Mark 10:29-31, we are reminded that suffering is not necessarily an adverse factor in our lives. It can be for our benefit or blessing. Our true character is tested with trials but our perseverance in these times builds character which, in turn, produces hope. Growing in character isn't an instantaneous process. There are no microwaves for patience. There's no instant pot for joy. Gentleness doesn't come in a foil pouch where you just add hot water. Growing your character is a process that the Holy Spirit oversees, often using the most difficult things in our lives as sculpting tools.

MY PRAYER

God, teach me to be patient and to put my complete trust in you. Help me to build my faith and recognize the areas where you want me to grow and develop so that I am ready for all that you have planned for my life. I pray for these things in the name of your son, Jesus Christ. Amen.

READ: PROVERBS 3:5-6

QUESTION #1: What are you feeling impatient about in this season of your life?

QUESTION #2: In what areas do you believe that God is wanting you to grow and develop?

CONTEMPLATE

Create a list of things in life that can't be achieved instantly. Create a list of things that can be achieved instantly. Which do you think are most valuable?

DEMONSTRATING GRACE

All this is evidence that God's judgment is right, and as a result you will be counted worthy of the kingdom of God, for which you are suffering. God is just: He will pay back trouble to those who trouble you and give relief to you who are troubled, and to us as well. This will happen when the Lord Jesus is revealed from heaven in blazing fire with his powerful angels.
(2 Thessalonians 1:5-7)

If you read much about the life of the apostle Paul, you will see that Satan challenged him with many trials. From imprisonment to shipwrecks to severe beatings, Paul's faith was tested over and over. To his credit and the glory of God, Paul endured and grew stronger in his faith as a result of these trials. Paul proved himself to be well-suited and worthy of God's grace. Through the Bible, we learn of the testing of Job, Abraham, Joseph, Daniel, Moses, David, Isaiah, and King David. Though it may not seem intuitive, we should, perhaps, consider it an honor to be tested in these ways.

Great faith is often formed by the resistance we encounter to that faith. When we don't give up or retreat, we gain what has been promised to us through God's Word. God entrusts us with these small trials for his glory. When others see how we respond to these trials, they will know that God is at work within us. We can demonstrate our relationship with God by how we respond to the trials. Our worthiness will be measured accordingly. If we react by complaining, indulging in self-pity or seeking sympathy, we do not honor God. We must not lose sight of the manner in which Christ suffered for our sins.

In 1 Peter 3:18, we are reminded that Christ endured the cross to cover our sins, sickness, and poverty. We were made worthy by the death, burial, and resurrection of Christ. Because of this sacrifice, we can receive and believe in Him. Our hope must be centered around Christ. He will carry us through the darkest storms in our lives. When we rely upon him and show joy in our suffering, we broadcast his glory, goodness, and faithfulness to the watching world.

MY PRAYER

Heavenly Father, thank you for increasing my strength with every trial. May I speak peace into every storm that comes my way. Let the solutions I'm looking for always be found in your Son. I pray for these things in the name of Jesus. Amen.

READ: PHILIPPIANS 1:29-30

QUESTION #1: Recall a time when you were able to demonstrate God's grace in the midst of a storm. How did that experience shape your faith and relationship with God?

QUESTION #2: In what ways can you teach others to persevere through trials by leaning into God's grace?

CONTEMPLATE

Describe a time in your life when you believe your maturity and faith were being tested. How are you different as a result of this trial?

CARPE DIEM

Concerning the coming of our Lord Jesus Christ and our being gathered to him, we ask you, brothers and sisters, not to become easily unsettled or alarmed by the teaching allegedly from us—whether by a prophecy or by word of mouth or by letter—asserting that the day of the Lord has already come. Don't let anyone deceive you in any way, for that day will not come until the rebellion occurs and the man of lawlessness is revealed, the man doomed to destruction. (2 Thessalonians 2:1-3)

There was great consternation and confusion among the Thessalonians about the second coming of Christ. Some believed that the return of Christ was imminent. As time elapsed, they grew impatient. As the persecution of Christians continued, they lost hope. In his letter, Paul did his best to correct the misinformation, much of which was being spread by false prophets and those who wanted to discourage these new Christians. In the end, Paul acknowledges that the date and time of Jesus' return is known only to God and not a relevant matter for Christians. We are instead encouraged to live every day as if it were our last, living exemplary lives that honor God. Whether Christ is coming tomorrow or 1,000 years from now, there are things that we should be doing today in anticipation of his return.

In Hebrews 9:28, we get affirmation that Christ will appear again to bring salvation to those who are eagerly awaiting him. Paul encourages us to also be eager in our anticipation and to adopt a sense of urgency in developing our spiritual gifts and purifying our lives from the sin that separates us from God. At the same time, we should exercise patience, acknowledging that God's timing is not our timing. Perhaps the order of events will not suit our personal timelines, but we should not lose hope.

There's one thing that we can be absolutely certain about. Jesus will come again to save the living and the dead who have placed their faith in him.

When Jesus was explaining how the Son of Man would one day return to his disciples, he used The Parable of The Talents (Matthew 24-25) to illustrate his point. More than just waiting on Christ to return, Jesus wanted his disciples to be good stewards of the resources he had entrusted to them. There was much work to be done. Like the servants who invested their gold for the Master's benefit, there would be a great reward. For the servant who played it safe, the outcome would not be good. God wants us to use our time to proclaim the Gospel and spread his word. He also wants us to encourage other Christians and lead them to a more fulfilling relationship with Christ. As true believers, we should live each day as if Christ were returning tomorrow.

MY PRAYER
God, let me live each day as if it were my last. Give me both patience and a sense of eagerness while I wait for your triumphant return. Let me use these last days in a way that benefits your Kingdom and shines a light for others to see. I pray for these things in the name of your son, Jesus Christ. Amen.

READ: MATTHEW 25:1-30

QUESTION #1: If today were indeed your last day in this life, what piece of unfinished business would you want to take care of?

QUESTION #2: How are you investing the gifts you've been given for the benefit of God's Kingdom?

CONTEMPLATE

Write about the things you would feel compelled to do if you knew that Christ was returning in 10 days. Prioritize each item. What is keeping you from acting on this list today?

"So then, brothers and sisters, stand firm and hold fast to the teachings we passed on to you, whether by word of mouth or by letter."

(2 Thessalonians 2:15)

WEEK 6

CONFIDENCE IN GOD'S POWER

"... and all the ways that wickedness deceives those who are perishing. They perish because they refused to love the truth and so be saved. For this reason God sends them a powerful delusion so that they will believe the lie and so that all will be condemned who have not believed the truth but have delighted in wickedness." (2 Thessalonians 2:10-12)

God is of infinite power. *We know that he can do all things and that no purpose of his can be thwarted (Job 42:2.)* We read of God's power throughout the Bible starting with the very act of creation, to giving Abraham and Sara a child, to flooding the earth, parting the Red Sea and the various miracles performed through Jesus and his disciples throughout the New Testament. We also know of his power over Satan. God has power over everything Satan does. In Luke 10:19, we are reminded that we have been delegated the power and authority over the enemy. For these reasons and more, Paul wants his readers to know that God, in the end, will deal with the non-believers, false prophets and those who reject the Gospel.

In 1 Timothy 2:3-4, we read "For this is good and acceptable in the sight of God our Savior, who desires all men to be saved and to come to the knowledge of the truth." It is true that God wants all of us to be saved, but he also knows that some of us will choose to believe the lies and deceptions of the devil. God puts the responsibility of pledging allegiance to his kingdom or the kingdom of darkness squarely on our shoulders. He allows us to accept the sacrifice made by Jesus on the cross or to reject the gift of salvation. God wants us to be fully committed. Just as there's no such thing as being a little pregnant, there is no middle ground when it comes to being saved. Either you are saved or you are lost.

As Christians, we can take comfort in knowing that God is always more than fair with us. He may give us trials, but he also gives us an abundance of grace and mercy. In Ephesians 2:8-10, we are reminded that God's grace has allowed us to be saved through our faith and that this is a gift from God, not as a result of anything we did on our own. God made us for good works. Too many men sit on the fence in regards to their relationship with Christ, keeping one foot firmly planted in their comfortable life of sin while dipping the other foot in the fresh water of a Christ-centered life. What is stopping you from accepting the gift of God's salvation and embracing the fact that Christ paid for your sins on the cross?

MY PRAYER

God, give me the wisdom to be ever mindful of your awesome power over the universe. Let me be fully committed to you both in thought and in action. Let me do all I can to save my brothers by bringing them to a life that honors you. I pray for these things in the name of your son, Jesus Christ. Amen.

READ: JOHN 3:18-21

QUESTION #1: If someone could observe every aspect of your life for a week, would they describe you as someone fully committed to Christ or someone on the fence?

QUESTION #2: What keeps you from being 100 percent committed to God?

CONTEMPLATE

Think of a friend who may not be fully committed to God. In what ways will you encourage this person to surrender? What aspect of your life serves as evidence of God's grace and mercy?

GOD'S IMPERFECT VESSEL

But we ought always to thank God for you, brothers and sisters loved by the Lord, because God chose you as first fruits to be saved through the sanctifying work of the Spirit and through belief in the truth. He called you to this through our gospel, that you might share in the glory of our Lord Jesus Christ. (2 Thessalonians 2:13-14)

God's plan for growing his Kingdom on this earth seems counter-intuitive at first glance. Paul tells us that we have an obligation, as Christians, to share the good news of God's Kingdom with others. Not only will proclaiming the Gospel bring joy to our lives, but it also brings glory to God. Part of my personal journey has been hampered by of my lack of confidence in my ability to defend truths that are difficult for people to comprehend, especially non-believers. Why would God depend on a wounded, imperfect sinner like me to tell his story and the promise of salvation? After all, wouldn't a few modern-day miracles be way more effective in bringing new followers into the fold? I won't pretend to fully understand God's nature, but I've often wondered if this is the answer: God wants us to feel inclined to grow spiritually and motivated to live exemplary lives. He wants us to gain the wisdom needed to make the message clear.

In 1 Peter 3:15, we are reminded to revere Christ and to tell others the reason for our hope. We must remain alert to the opportunities to share the Gospel whether it happens in the grocery store, on the golf course, or over a cup of coffee with a coworker. We must be able to share God's truth in a logical and compelling manner with a strong sense of humility. Non-believers are more likely to respond to an approach that relies on patience and understanding. More than just a conversation, the process likely depends on the example that you have modeled as a Christian. You will be challenged and asked tough questions. Respond with patience and gentleness. Admit when you don't know the answers.

In Matthew 28:18-20, Jesus shares with his disciples the "Great Commission" calling them to go out and make disciples of all the nations, teaching others about the Kingdom of God and all that comes from living a life that honors God. We can rely on the Holy Spirit to give us the words and confidence we need to act in faith. He is preparing the hearts of those who come into our lives looking for a relationship with Christ. We are, indeed, imperfect vessels for such a high calling and God would have it no other way. When people learn the reason for our joy and hope, they will want to know more about becoming part of God's chosen few.

MY PRAYER

God, thank you for the trust you have placed in me to share your word and to bring you glory. I am an imperfect vessel but I know that your grace is sufficient for me. My weakness is made perfect in your power. Give me the courage to recognize and seize upon every opportunity to bring others to you. I pray for these things in the name of your son, Jesus Christ. Amen.

READ: MATTHEW 28:18-20

QUESTION #1: What prevents you from sharing the Gospel with others?

QUESTION #2: How can you better model how a Christian should live his or her life?

CONTEMPLATE

Make a list of your friends who do not know Jesus. How will you pray for them in the next few days? How will you approach sharing the Gospel with them?

HOLD FAST

So then, brothers and sisters, stand firm and hold fast to the teachings we passed on to you, whether by word of mouth or by letter. (2 Thessalonians 2:15)

I remember when my sons were young, they launched a relentless crusade to convince me that our family would always be incomplete without a puppy in our home. At the time I remember thinking how difficult it was to manage a home with two small children, adding a rambunctious four-legged creature would only add to the chaos. I gave in. When they became pre-teens, they couldn't imagine being the only kids in the "whole middle school" without an iPhone. It was a ridiculous request. But, of course, I gave in. As I became older, I became wiser. When they begged for televisions in each of their rooms, I finally stood firm. "Absolutely not!" I was told that I was a mean, horrible, and stingy person but, nonetheless, I stood firm. I'm proud to say that after many failed attempts as a parent, I finally drew the line and held fast to my convictions. Now that my children are grown, I still struggle with the art of following my convictions. The same is true for my Christian beliefs and values.

In Isaiah 7:9, the prophet Isaiah told King Ahaz that if he would not stand firm in his faith, he will not stand at all. The same is true for us. I've now spent several years studying God's Word and the principles of leading a Christ-centered life. I've only recently discovered that as important as it may be to know the truth presented in God's Word, it's even more important to hold on to it. As sure as life itself, we will be challenged in our faith. Satan knows exactly what to target and when to attack us. If we are standing firm on the rock of Jesus, we won't be moved.

Perhaps the best way to stand firm in Christ is to do so in communion with others. It's as simple as surrounding yourself with other believers who will hold you accountable for your words and actions. You've heard the phrase, "there's strength in numbers." It's true. Find a group of friends who have your permission to ask you questions about your faith or your Christian walk. Become committed to meeting with a small group of other guys who are most likely experiencing the same type of temptations you are facing. Do not fight your battles alone. The devil likes to separate us from other Christians like a wolf separates a lamb from the flock. When we go into isolation, we become easy prey for Satan.

MY PRAYER

God, give me the conviction to stand firm in my faith. Let me build my house on the rock that is Jesus. When challenges come my way, give me the courage to recognize Satan's work and to push back, resisting temptation, anxiety, and discouragement. I pray for these things in the name of your son, Jesus Christ. Amen.

READ: 1 CORINTHIANS 16:13-14

QUESTION #1: In what areas of your life do you have the most difficulty standing firm for Christ?

QUESTION #2: What are the temptations you face when you are isolated from others?

CONTEMPLATE

Recall a time in your life when you experienced regret over not standing firm on a particular issue. What were the factors that caused you to give in? What were the consequences of not standing by your convictions?

STAY BUSY

In the name of the Lord Jesus Christ, we command you, brothers and sisters, to keep away from every believer who is idle and disruptive and does not live according to the teaching you received from us. For you yourselves know how you ought to follow our example. We were not idle when we were with you, nor did we eat anyone's food without paying for it. On the contrary, we worked night and day, laboring and toiling so that we would not be a burden to any of you. We did this, not because we do not have the right to such help, but in order to offer ourselves as a model for you to imitate. For even when we were with you, we gave you this rule: "The one who is unwilling to work shall not eat." (2 Thessalonians 3:6-10)

The widely-used phrase, "you reap what you sow" may have its roots in Paul's letter to the Thessalonians. In his efforts to set an example, Paul worked day and night while he was with them. In addition to his ministry work, Paul supported himself by working as a tentmaker. When he received word that some members of his new church were refusing to work because they claimed to be waiting for the return of Christ. Paul rebuked them and made it clear that any able-bodied man who did not work, did not deserve to eat. It sounds harsh to modern ears, but Paul understood that in God's providence, only those who work deserve the reward at the end of the journey. Freeloaders endanger a community by taking without giving anything in return.

Jesus' teachings on the value and purpose of work were very clear. Work is a very important element of Christian life. Our work ethic is a testament to others, particularly when we work cheerfully and without complaint. In Ephesians 6:7-8, we are called to work as if we are doing so in service to God, rather than man. We know that God will reward us for the good that we do. Paul's efforts and sacrifices made on behalf of God's Kingdom were not a necessary evil, they were an expression of God's love.

Laziness and sloth are condemned on 14 separate occasions in Proverbs, but this doesn't mean that rest is wrong. Laziness is the refusal to work. Rest is the refusal to be a workaholic. In Matthew 11:28, Jesus invites all who labor to come to him for the gift of rest. Even though God was all powerful and did not need rest, he wanted to set an example for us. At the moment of creation, he gave us the Sabbath to rest following six days of labor. While our labor is important, the same is true for our rest and rejuvenation. The work we do brings honor and glory to God but the quality time we invest in our loved ones is also an important factor to living a Christ-centered life.

MY PRAYER

Father, God, let my work be a testament of my honor and duty in serving your Kingdom. Give me purpose and meaning in the work I do so that I can find fulfillment and joy, regardless of the rigor involved. I pray for these things in the name of your son, Jesus Christ. Amen.

READ: COLOSSIANS 3:23-24

QUESTION #1: How does your work ethic show the Kingdom of God to people around you?

QUESTION #2: In what way can your Sabbath time be used for the benefit of God's Kingdom?

CONTEMPLATE

Make a list of your daily and weekly activities that are done solely for the benefit of others. What portion of your week involves activities that serve God? What prevents you from improving this ratio?

TOUGH LOVE

*Take special note of anyone who does not obey our instruction in this
letter. Do not associate with them, in order that they may feel ashamed.
Yet do not regard them as an enemy, but warn them as you would a fellow
believer. (2 Thessalonians 3:14-15)*

I remember when my wife and I first became parents, we were
overwhelmed by the responsibility of trying to figure out the best
way to raise our two sons. As the recipient of corporal punishment
as a youth, I struggled to find the balance between acknowledging my
children's inappropriate behavior and my fear of crushing their self-esteem
and understanding of my unconditional love for them. We became big
fans of an approach to parenting called Conscious Discipline. One of the
primary principles of this philosophy is teaching children the difference
between "good choices" and "bad choices" and that there are consequences
associated with every choice they make. Though many years have passed,
I have found that the same is true for the choices we make as adults. As
Christians, we will encounter fellow believers who continue to make bad
choices in their lives. When this happens, we have an obligation to speak
truth into their lives without judging or withholding our love for them.

In Hebrews 12:11, we read, *"No discipline seems pleasant at the time,
but painful. Later on, however, it produces a harvest of righteousness
and peace for those who have been trained by it."* When we shield fellow
believers from the consequences of their mistakes, we deny them an
opportunity to grow in the fellowship of God. By not holding them
responsible for their behavior, we deny them the happy, healthy, and
fulfilling life they could have by living a life that honors God, and put
their souls at risk. God separates the sheep from the goats. We must take
an active role in setting those we love on a path toward redemption.

But Paul warns us that we must be careful how we do this. We cannot treat our fellow believers as enemies. When we admonish the behavior of others, we must do so in a spirit of love, lest our words be perceived as judgmental. The last thing we want to do is make a wayward Christian who has strayed feel like an outcast. We must do all we can to maintain a kinship so that we can restore them to the fellowship of Christ. If you're like me, you don't always respond to a gentle tap on the shoulder. Sometimes I need a swift kick in the hindquarters. No matter how hard the kick, if it is done with love and genuine concern, our chances of getting someone back on the right track have far greater chances for lasting success.

MY PRAYER

God, I am thankful for the many people who have made the difficult choice to help me get my life back on track. Let me exercise that same sense of genuine concern and love to others who have wandered away from you. Let me be intentional in doing so with a sincere heart. I pray for these things in the name of your son, Jesus Christ. Amen.

READ: HEBREWS 12:4-13

QUESTION #1: Is there someone in your life who might benefit from a gentle tap on the shoulder?

QUESTION #2: In what area of your life might you, yourself, benefit from a dose of tough love?

CONTEMPLATE

Recall a time when someone rebuked you for what they considered to be bad behavior. How did you respond? Looking back, what did you learn from that experience that might make you more effective in helping a loved one get back on the right track?

15 RULES OF ENGAGEMENT FOR SMALL-GROUP STUDIES

1. Nothing said in the group gets discussed outside the group!

2. Be transparent. Be authentic. Be your true self.

3. Everyone needs to share, both as a speaker and a listener.

4. Encourage one another. Speak truth into each others' lives avoiding the temptation to "fix" each other.

5. Challenge each other. It's reasonable to disagree, but respect boundaries.

6. Give your darkest issues the light of day. It's incredibly liberating!

7. Be willing to be vulnerable. Take a chance and let your risk be rewarded.

8. We all have blind spots. Dare to explore your own.

9. Absolutely NO gossip.

10. Embrace your mistakes. Take ownership of your weaknesses, knowing that we're all human.

11. Resist the urge to rescue others when they struggle to find the right words. Let people finish their thoughts.

12. Don't be afraid of silence. Pause and feel the weight of what has been shared.

13. Trust is our most important currency. Earn it and then be willing to extend trust to others.

14. Side conversations are not allowed; only one voice at a time.

15. When possible, find time to connect with each other outside the small group setting.

IS THE RAPTURE REAL?

BY PATRICK MILLER

What is the Rapture? Pop culture references like the Left Behind series paint a picture of a sudden, apocalyptic reality where people all over the world vanish. Planes crash because their pilots are gone. Little kids can't find their moms. And if you are one of those "left behind," then you can be sure that something even worse is coming for you.

The Rapture is a future event when Jesus returns to gather all Christians who believe in him and take them to heaven. Then, after seven years, he will come back again and establish his millennial kingdom. During that seven years, those who were not taken away by Jesus will suffer "tribulations"—hardship and trials as punishment for their sins.

To tip my hand: this is not a theological perspective I subscribe to (mainly because I don't think it can be found in the Bible). I don't believe the Rapture is real.

So why talk about it?

HOW THE END AFFECTS YOUR PRESENT

Your view of the end times matters. Why? Because what you believe about the end of the story impacts how you live right now.

If you think the earth and its non-Christian inhabitants
are destined only for trials and tribulations, you won't have
any reason to invest in earthly things. There's no point in
saving for retirement. Or recycling to reduce the use of
non-renewable resources. Or being employed as anything
other than a missionary. In the end, it's all destined for the
tribulation dumpster fire.

Rapture theology trains people to not care about the world
around them. But that's not what Jesus taught.

In his great prayer, Jesus didn't pray, "Take me heaven on your
Rapture train." Instead, he prayed for God's kingdom to come
down to earth. "On earth as it is in heaven."

WHY PEOPLE THINK THE RAPTURE IS REAL

Those who believe in the Rapture do so because it's what they've
been taught in church. Rapture theology is an American
theological innovation. Before 200 years ago, no one would
have understood it. Since then, it's been popularized by
reference Bibles, movies, and books. It's easy to take it for
granted as biblical truth, even though it's nowhere in the Bible.

Of course, some people will contend that it is. Let's look at two
passages that people turn to in order to prove that the Rapture
is real. What do you think?

MATTHEW 24

As it was in the days of Noah, so it will be at the coming of
the Son of Man. For in the days before the flood, people were

eating and drinking, marrying and giving in marriage, up to the day Noah entered the ark; and they knew nothing about what would happen until the flood came and took them all away. That is how it will be at the coming of the Son of Man. Two men will be in the field; one will be taken and the other left. Two women will be grinding with a hand mill; one will be taken and the other left. (Read Matthew 24:37-21)

According to Rapture theology, you want to be like the people taken away, not the people left behind. Unfortunately, this reads the story backward.

Jesus is comparing his return to the days of Noah. You know who you didn't want to be in the days of Noah? The people who were taken away by the raging floodwaters!

As Jesus said, "They didn't know what would happen until the flood came and took them all away."

Do you know who you should want to be? The people left behind after the flood, like Noah and his family. Jesus isn't talking about a Rapture. He's talking about the final judgment. And at that time, it's good to be left behind.

1 THESSALONIANS 4

For the Lord himself will come down from heaven, with a loud command, with the voice of the archangel and with the trumpet call of God, and the dead in Christ will rise first. After that, we who are still alive and are left will be caught up together with them in the clouds to meet the Lord in the air.

And so we will be with the Lord forever.

1 THESSALONIANS 4:16-17

This is the classic Rapture passage. If you already have Rapture theology in your head, you're probably thinking, "See? You just proved the point. Rapture."

But that's a case of confirmation bias. If you didn't already believe in a Rapture, you'd never conclude that this passage is describing Jesus coming down to take people back to heaven.

Why not? Because in this passage, Jesus comes down, and he doesn't go back up again. Absolutely nothing in the passage says that Jesus is going back to heaven.

A common objection is to ask, "What about the people who are meeting with the Lord in the air? Aren't they going to heaven?" No. In the Bible, "the air" is never synonymous with "heaven." In this case, "the air" is halfway between heaven (where Jesus started) and earth (where Jesus is going).

This would have made sense to Paul's original audience because they understood how cities were supposed to greet incoming kings. In Rome, when emperors approached a city, crowds would leave the city, meet the king outside the gates, and then usher him back in.

The Bible actually shows this. When Jesus comes to Jerusalem as a king on Palm Sunday, people leave Jerusalem to greet him and usher him into the city.

The believers in this passage aren't going to heaven. They're meeting Jesus halfway between heaven and earth, in the air, to usher Jesus to earth in a victorious procession. Jesus isn't SpaceX ship landing briefly from the skies, only to take off again. He's a king coming to execute his final judgment on the living and the dead.

BELIEF IN THE RAPTURE CAN MAKE LIFE HARDER
One problem with Rapture theology is that it implies that good Christians escape tribulations in this world. This is why Jesus Raptures believers: to protect them from future hardship.

This is pretty much the opposite of what the Bible says. Jesus taught that in this world, we will always have trouble (John 16:33). And Paul says that we enter into the kingdom of God through the tribulations of this world (Acts 14:22).

If Christians are misled into believing that God will keep them from the hard times of this life, they won't be equipped to follow God when the hard times come. Some Christians are surprised and shaken when tribulations hit. They wonder, "Why is God letting this happen to me?" as though their suffering undermines the truth of God's goodness and sovereignty.

But Jesus says that God's kingdom comes to earth when Christians experience hardship and persecution but respond with faith, trust, and love. When we endure tribulations this way, we show the watching world that our hope is in something bigger, better, and more powerful than the worst trials this world can throw at us.

Reprinted by permission of Patrick Miller.

FredParry.Life

Becoming The Man God Intended You To Be

Want to offer feedback?

Write to Fred Parry,
711 West Broadway, Columbia, Missouri 65203
or email fparry61@gmail.com.

www.FredParry.Life

Other Books By Fred Parry

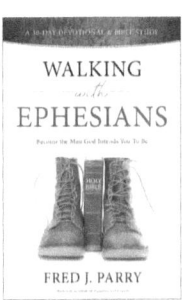
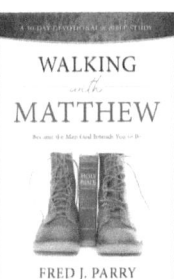
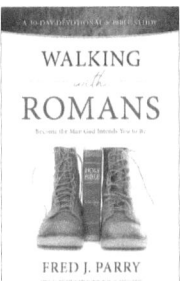

TAKE THE BARNABAS CHALLENGE

For God did not appoint us to suffer wrath but to receive salvation through our Lord Jesus Christ. He died for us so that, whether we are awake or asleep, we may live together with him. Therefore encourage one another and build each other up, just as in fact you are doing. (1 Thessalonians 5:9-11, NIV)

You can read about Barnabas in the Acts of the Apostles. He was one of the apostles of the early church who traveled with Paul on his first missionary trip. We also know that he was a tireless worker and was generous in his financial support of the church. But more importantly, Barnabas was someone who was known as a great encourager. In fact, Barnabas' birth name was Joseph, but his fellow apostles called him Barnabas, which meant "Son of Encouragement."

It's been a tough few years and, as a result, men are more discouraged right now than at any point in our history. With escalating suicide rates, drug overdoses, and men retreating from their families, it's time for us, as men, to step up and find ways to encourage our brothers who are struggling.

Maybe it's a family member, a co-worker, or a complete stranger who may be down on his luck. Maybe it's your neighbor or a guy you see at the gym once a week. You can imagine what it's like right now to be a police officer, a paramedic, or a teacher. Your simple words of encouragement or gratitude could be a real game-changer for another man.

When we encourage another man, our words lift his heart towards God. More than simply responding to dire circumstances with empathy, we also should go the extra step of offering hope and encouragement.

Often, the best gift we can give another man is an ear to listen and the time to let him know that he is not alone in his struggles.

The Barnabas Challenge is as simple as this. All you have to do is encourage one man a day, every day, for the next 30 days. Think about a man who might need your encouragement right now. The Barnabas Challenge is as easy as sending an email, text message, or handwritten note. Maybe it's just a pat on the back or lending an ear to listen at the end of a difficult day.

I hope you'll consider taking this one step further. What if each of us could encourage five of our own friends to also take this challenge? Think about it. In less than a month, your small gesture will have touched the lives of 180 men who might need it NOW more than ever.

And when the guys we touch start paying it forward, there's no telling how big of a difference we can make. Our goal is to encourage one million men but none of us should be surprised if God has bigger plans for the Barnabas Challenge.

It's really just that simple but this effort has to begin with YOU!

Scan the QR Code and get started today!